Ireland's Ancient Stones

A Megalithic Heritage

Kenneth McNally

Appletree Press

First published in 2006
by Appletree Press
The Old Potato Station
14 Howard Street South
Belfast
BT7 1AP

Tel: +44 (0) 28 90 24 30 74
Fax: +44 (0) 28 90 24 67 56
E-mail: reception@appletree.ie
Web-site: www.appletree.ie

A catalogue record for this book is available from the British Library.

Ireland's Ancient Stones – A Megalithic Heritage

ISBN-10: 0-86281-996-2
ISBN-13: 978-0-86281-996-5

Desk & Marketing Editor: Jean Brown
Copy-Editor: Jim Black
Designer: Stuart Wilkinson
Production Manager: Paul McAvoy

9 8 7 6 5 4 3 2 1

AP3312

CONTENTS

PREFACE

In 1849 an Oxford academic named Algernon Herbert combined two Greek words, *megas*, meaning great, and *lithos*, stone, thus coining 'megalithic', a word which has always seemed to me imbued with potent imagery. Behind the prosaic definition lies a misty prehistoric world into which these remarkable monuments can provide a tantalising glimpse. The Irish countryside is rich in tangible reminders of a far off past that is very much part of the present, and we can learn a great deal about our distant ancestors by visiting these peaceful sites and contemplating their ancient stones.

Herbert could scarcely have foreseen the significance of his inspiration. The word megalithic was soon taken up by others and eventually entered the literature as a serviceable generic term to describe a wide variety of Neolithic and Bronze Age monuments built of large stones. Without it, archaeology would seem a less colourful science.

Part of the fascination of these monuments lies in their often astonishing size and sophistication, prompting questions about how and why they were constructed, and also in the skilful use of natural stone to fashion something that is intrinsically pleasing to the eye. One only has to catch sight of a dolmen with its great poised capstone looming against the sky, to appreciate the vigorous architectural statement its builders toiled to achieve four thousand years ago. Even a simple standing stone, boldly faceted and encrusted with lichen, can possess the tactile quality of a piece of modern sculpture.

This book is the outcome of visits to a great many sites throughout the country over several years. Its approach is frankly idiosyncratic, and I have tended towards those lesser-known antiquities, often located in out of the way places not always easy of access, rather than the more familiar and much publicised ones of tourist renown. I have however included a number of the latter to maintain a balance: the fine dolmens of Poulnabrone and Legananny are here; so too the elaborate court tombs of Annaghmare, Creevykeel and Magheraghanrush, as well as Drombeg Stone Circle and the Long Stone of Punchestown. It would have been remiss to have bypassed the magnificent passage tomb of Newgrange; no one who visits this most celebrated and written about of all Irish prehistoric monuments will be disappointed, even though they will find themselves sharing the experience with many of the several hundred others who are daily ushered through its wonders.

It is, then, mainly to the quieter places that I have been drawn in search of the strange and unexpected: the legendary Cúchulainn's Stone; neglected dolmens with colourful names like Tawnatruffaun, Kilrooskagh and Gortavern; the curious Masonbrook Ring and the pagan idol of Crom Cruaich...

'And somehow you're sick of the highway
with its noise and its easy needs
And you seek the risk of the byway
And you reck not where it leads.'

(Robert Service – '*The Lone Trail*')

Those intent on exploring among the byways will find the excellent *Discovery* series of maps published by the Ordnance Survey invaluable. Produced to a scale of 1:50 000, they cover the entire country in great detail and mark monuments of every kind. Even thus equipped, reaching one's goal is not always easy. The majority of megaliths are uncared for, often concealed by gorse and brambles or situated amid tracts of inscrutable peat bog. Others merge invisibly into the background on boulder-strewn hillsides (so a good pair of binoculars will prove useful). The expansion of state forestry over large areas of countryside in recent years has added to the difficulty of locating many upland sites, while an unwelcome side effect is the loss of fine views formerly to be enjoyed from them.

An increasing number of sites are coming under state care as designated National Monuments, though even then signposting is sometimes inadequate or lacking altogether. The fact that a monument is signposted does not necessarily imply a right of way. Access to many involves crossing private property and where this is evident the permission of the landowner should be sought as a matter of courtesy. It will seldom be refused. Trespass notices are rare in Ireland and farmers are generally tolerant of visitors who observe the countryside code and exercise due care.

It will by now be evident that seeking out these intriguing monuments is not a pursuit likely to recommend itself to those tied to a schedule. Hopefully today's venturers on the megalithic trail will not find themselves in a similar predicament to Gabriel Beranger, an intrepid eighteenth-century antiquary who embarked on a sketching survey of field monuments in the west of Ireland in the summer of 1779. The following incident, as recorded in his diary, borders on pure farce, but it will also serve as a cautionary tale for the unwary.

"June 9th. Set out with Colonel Irwin, interpreter, and servants on horseback, to draw a famous cromleac, called 'Finmacool's Griddle,' situated in a bog ten miles long, and about three broad. Took two guides on the verge of said bog. Went by various windings, until arrived at a small hill, on which this old monument is fixed. Drew a plan; but Mr. Irwin, looking at his watch, and seeing dinner-time approach, asked our guides for a short cut to go to Fortland—which he knew there was. They seemed ignorant of it, but undertook to try and find it out. We followed, when, all of a sudden my horse sunk under me in the bog. This stopped us; and, as he could not get out, the guides were sent for assistance and spades to dig him out. We left our interpreter and servants on the spot; and the Colonel, trusting to his memory, undertook to guide me, and we set forward on foot, making many zig-zags on the worst ground I ever trod on, sinking at every step half-way up my boots and being obliged to walk, or rather run, pretty fast, for fear of sinking. After an hour's travelling, we could see nothing but the heavens and the bog, and the ground became softer and wetter, so that we could not advance without sinking in it. We tried to the right, then to the left, and twined and twined so much that we knew not which way to go, the Colonel having lost sight of his landmark. We continued moving on, as the Colonel told me that we should be lost if we ceased moving one moment. I confess here that I thought it my last day. The anxiety of the mind, the fatigue of the body, the insufferable heat of the day, and the intolerable thirst I felt, made me almost unable to proceed; but remembering that to stop a moment was instant death, I followed Mr. Irwin, putting my foot from where he withdrew his, as nearly as I could on the ground, which was now quite liquid, and appeared a lough to me. Two hours more were we in this situation, when Mr. Irwin got sight of some other mark, which gave me new courage; and little by little the ground grew firmer, and we made for some stacks of turf, and so forth on firm ground unto Fortland, where we arrived at seven, having been since three o'clock wandering in this horrid wilderness."

Beranger of course did not have the benefit of a reliable guide book on his rambles, whereas today's traveller is well served in that respect. The following are selected not only for their comprehensive listing of sites, but also for the historical perspective they provide.

Though it is long out of print and consequently not fully up to date with archaeological progress, Estyn Evans' *Prehistoric and Early Christian Ireland: A Guide* (London, 1966) remains an exemplary introduction to the ancient riches of the countryside and may be obtained from the larger libraries. Anthony Weir's *Early Ireland: A Field Guide* (Belfast, 1980) covers similar ground and is strong on megalithic remains. Those requiring information on a whole range of monuments, from prehistoric to late Mediaeval, will find Peter Harbison's *Guide to the National Monuments of Ireland* indispensable. The most recent edition has been expanded to include Northern Ireland and its usefulness is enhanced by a map section. The excellent *Historic Monuments of Northern Ireland* published by the Department of the Environment for Northern Ireland, is regrettably no longer available, but a new updated edition is in preparation at the time of writing and its appearance will be eagerly welcomed. *Sacred Ireland* by Cary Meehan (Glastonbury, 2002) is a unique travellers' guide to the ancient wonders and curiosities of the landscape, spiced with legend and folklore and personal comment. J.H. Brennan's *A Guide to Megalithic Ireland* (London, 1994) is a synoptic survey of sites in the Irish Republic only. One of the most enduring general guides is Sean P. O'Riordain's *Antiquities of the Irish Countryside*, first published in 1942 and frequently revised and reprinted. It is recommended reading both for the clarity of its presentation and for its extensive bibliography.

INTRODUCTION

According to archaeological evidence, man first arrived in Ireland around 10,000 years ago, some time after the last Ice Age ended. Land bridges that existed between Britain and Ireland were slowly submerged as the ice melted and the sea level rose, but it is possible that some remained long enough to allow the initial wave of colonists to cross over by this means. Those who followed later would have come by boat, probably in skin-covered craft not so very different from the currachs still used in the west of Ireland.

These Mesolithic (Middle Stone Age) immigrants lived by fishing, hunting and food gathering, leaving to this day traces of their campsites in the form of shell-middens and discarded flint tools. Their continual foraging for food necessitated a semi-nomadic existence, but they also occupied permanent habitation sites in some areas, such as those that have been identified at Mount Sandel near Coleraine, Lough Boora in Co. Offaly and on the flood-plain of the River Bann at Toomebridge.

The unprogressive Mesolithic way of life continued unchallenged for several thousand years, until the arrival around 4000 BC, perhaps somewhat earlier, of Neolithic (New Stone Age) settlers who introduced farming, and over time brought about far-reaching changes in the landscape, most notably through the clearance of large areas of woodland for the cultivation of crops and stock-rearing. Whatever initial conflict there may have been between the two groups must have given way to cooperation, and eventually the Mesolithic hunter-gatherers would have been converted to the discipline of an agricultural economy.

Doubtless, too, they would have looked with curiosity and awe at the great stone structures the newcomers built, in which the dead were buried with elaborate ritual. The concept of an afterlife was central to Neolithic culture, and the scale and sophistication of these sepulchral monuments is an indication of the time and labour lavished on their construction.

Megalithic tombs are broadly classified into two categories: gallery tombs, which embraces court tombs, portal tombs and wedge tombs; and passage tombs. Both types were built to accommodate multiple burials and are identified by the shape of the cairns which covered them. Gallery tombs are contained in oval or long tapered cairns, passage tombs have round cairns. In very many cases these large mounds of earth and stone have disappeared, leaving the burial chambers exposed.

Court tombs have long galleries segmented by jambs into a number of individual chambers in which were placed the cremated or, more rarely, inhumed burials. The most distinguishing feature, from which the type takes its name, is a symmetrical open space or court reserved for ceremonial use in front of the gallery, demarcated by upright slabs called orthostats. The court may be semi-circular (single court) or oval (full court) in plan: to the first the descriptive name 'horned cairn' has been given, while the second is sometimes referred to as a 'lobster-claw cairn', though these terms, coined in the early years of modern archaeology last century, are seldom used today.

Typically the court is located at one end of the cairn, to the east of the gallery, but variations are encountered in both of the types mentioned. Some tombs have two galleries opening inwards onto a central court, or, in reverse arrangement, the tomb may consist of two galleries set back to back with their forecourts facing outwards, creating a dual-court tomb, as at Audleystown in Co. Down. The orthostats of the court tend to be graded for height, with the most prominent stones placed on either side of the portals, or jambs, at the entrance to the gallery. In many instances the stones forming the court are set contiguously, but at other times they are spaced apart and linked by sections of dry-walling, known as 'post-and-panel' construction.

Court tombs predominate in the northern third of the country, with only a few isolated examples occurring elsewhere, suggesting perhaps that the initial influx of Neolithic colonists did not penetrate far beyond their points of entry. Court tombs in north-eastern counties generally have semi-circular forecourts – the classic Ulster 'horned-cairn' – while those in the west tend to be of more complex design on the full-court plan, and some have transeptal chambers opening off the gallery. Four hundred court tombs have been recorded and around one eighth of these have been excavated.

Where large mounds or cairns survive intact they frequently cover passage tombs. As the name implies, the tomb proper is accessed by a narrow lintel-roofed passage leading in from the side of the cairn. The plan of the chamber varies, but the classic Irish shape is cruciform, comprising a central area with three recesses opening off it. Newgrange at Brú na Bóinne in Co. Meath, is Ireland's best-known passage tomb, constructed about 3200 BC on a scale not witnessed elsewhere in western Europe at that time. Its beautifully decorated stones rank among the wonders of megalithic art, and the experience of entering the stillness of the great chamber is memorable.

The passage tomb builders had very definite ideas about the siting of these great monuments, nearly always choosing prominent hilltops which could be seen from afar. It seems that 'location, location, location' mattered, even in 3000 BC. Although all of these tombs are classed as megalithic, not all are necessarily built of large stones. Some have chambers constructed of dry-walling whose courses rise to meet a corbelled roof. This may be the result of cultural diversity, but could also have a practical reason, since the physical constraints of some of the more remote locations would have made it impossible to transport and erect very large blocks of stone.

Passage tombs sometimes occur in clusters – so-called megalithic cemeteries. Two miles west of Sligo at Carrowmore is the largest concentration of megaliths in Ireland, comprising numerous small passage tombs of simple construction, their bold dolmen-like chambers contrasting with the sophistication of those in the east of the country. Another passage tomb cemetery, Carrowkeel, also in Co. Sligo, is located on a series of stark limestone ridges in the forlorn Bricklieve Mountains to the west of Lough Arrow. There are fourteen cairns, not all of which contain typical passage tombs: one elongated example appears to have affinities with the court tombs, suggesting a blend of cultural traditions. The site has given its name to a type of pottery vessel known as Carrowkeel Ware.

Portal tombs, popularly called 'dolmens' (from the Breton word for a stone table), are single-chamber tombs. They are numerous in the northern counties of Sligo, Donegal, Down and Tyrone, and some fine monuments occur in south-east Ireland. In its basic form a portal tomb has a chamber constructed of tall orthostats, across the tops of which rests a large covering slab or capstone. Some of the simplest and at the same time most striking specimens consist of just three uprights and a capstone, and are designated 'tripod dolmens'. It is usual for the matched front supports to stand higher than the backstone, thereby giving the capstone its characteristic uptilt and accentuating the entrance. There sometimes remains in position between the portal stones a tall doorstone which closes the chamber; in some cases a low sillstone serves the same purpose. Capstones can be massive (one at Browne's Hill in Co. Carlow weighs an unprecedented 100 tons) and their emplacement must have entailed considerable labour and ingenuity. It was probably accomplished by hauling the stone up an earthen ramp constructed behind the chamber, using a system of levers and wooden rollers.

To these eye-catching structures country folk have given a variety of colourful names: 'giant's grave' and 'druid's altar' are among the most frequent and are self explanatory. 'Dermot and Grania's Bed' recalls the fugitive lovers of Celtic mythology, who in their flight from a vengeful king had to construct a bed of stones each night. Then there are specific local names: 'Ossian's Grave', 'The Giant's Load', 'Crawtree Stone', 'The Labby Rock', 'Kempe Stones' and so on. Many Ulster dolmens are, with blunt Northern pragmatism, called simply *cloghogle* – 'raised stone'.

Placing these structures in their correct chronological sequence poses problems. Their simple albeit dramatic form could be interpreted as belonging to the early phase of tomb building, and this opinion was shared by many archaeologists in the past. Latterly, however, this view has been changing and the evidence now seems to point to portal tombs having appeared towards the end of the Neolithic period. They may be degenerate versions of the court tombs, to which they seem to be related. It is tempting to regard them as representing a late resurgence of the megalithic tradition in people who no longer built in the sophisticated manner of the court and passage tombs.

Towards the close of the Neolithic a new type of gallery tomb made its appearance and continued to be built in the Bronze Age. This was the wedge tomb, recognised by its tapered shape, which decreases in width and height from west to east and is contained in a short, usually oval, cairn. The tomb entrance takes the form of a small antechamber, separated by jambs and sill from the main chamber, behind which there is sometimes a closed end chamber. A feature peculiar to wedge tombs is the double-walling of the gallery.

Wedge tombs predominate in western districts, but are well represented throughout Ireland. Around five hundred and fifty are known, many of these in the Burren region of Co. Clare, where the lithology contributed to a symmetry of construction not usually achieved elsewhere. The people who built the wedge tombs probably settled first in the copper-rich lands of West Munster, whose mineral deposits they may have exploited for commerce. Their culture is sometimes called Bell-beaker, after the decorated pottery that has been found in these tombs.

While the custom of building large and elaborate tombs declined in the Bronze Age, this period saw the appearance of another type of monument that would keep the megalithic tradition well and truly alive: the mysterious rings of standing stones that have long puzzled archaeologist and layman alike. Stone circles are not an exclusively Bronze Age monument: some may date from late Neolithic times and it is probable that a few were still being erected, or at least used, in the early Iron Age; but the majority seem to fit within a broadly 1500-year span starting around the end of the third millennium BC.

The visitor to any of the two hundred or so stone circles known in Ireland, whether large imposing monuments like The Lios at Lough Gur in Co. Limerick, or the diminutive five-stone rings found in Co. Kerry, can scarcely fail to wonder about their cryptic purpose. It is a subject capable of stimulating endless debate since, unlike the great tombs, there is no obvious explanation for the existence of these most enigmatic of prehistoric monuments. Theories abound, from pragmatic reasoning that they were places of assembly and law-making, to extravagant flights of fancy involving alien spacecraft. It has also been claimed that they served as astronomical observatories where druidic priests predicted lunar eclipses and other celestial phenomena. To see these structures as purpose-built observatories in a scientific sense is perhaps stretching credulity, but it is certainly possible that they had a more practical function as calendar stones, enabling farming communities to map the passage of the seasons. The arrangement of the stones themselves and the orientation of certain prominent ones suggest such a use, and in addition would not be inconsistent with the concept of the stone circle as a sanctuary where people whose lives were profoundly linked to the seasons and climate performed rites to ensure a fruitful harvest.

By definition, a stone circle is an arrangement of upright stones forming an open ring whose purpose was essentially ritual. Of the recorded sites two main concentrations are identified: in south-west Munster and mid-Ulster, the latter centred in the Sperrin Mountains region of Co. Tyrone. Here on the upland hill-slopes are numerous rings of low stones or boulders, occurring in proximity as inter-related groups, but for all that inconspicuous among the monotones of heathery moorland. Stone circles are also found in the adjoining counties of Fermanagh and Londonderry and here too the stones tend to be of small size, generally no more than 2-3 feet in height. Some of the Ulster circles have associated stone rows, called alignments, and some stand near cairns or other burial monuments. All these features are present at Beaghmore, a remarkable Bronze Age ceremonial site uncovered in Co. Tyrone in the 1940s.

Though, as has been observed, the majority of Ulster circles consist of relatively small stones, there are one or two notable exceptions. The fine monument at Ballynoe in the Lecale Peninsula is truly megalithic, several of its closely set orthostats standing to 6 feet or more in height. The circle is unusual in that it surrounds a burial mound, a combination which makes interpretation difficult.

The Munster distribution occurs mainly in two areas of Co. Cork: one in the coastal district of Ross Carbery and its hinterland, the other in the Boggeragh Mountains some 30 miles inland. There is a wealth of stone circles in the hilly country to the north of Coachford, as well as many standing stones and alignments. Here the circles are mostly of small diameter: Oughtihery 8½ feet, Rylane 11½ feet; but there are also some sizeable ones, like Loughatooma, an oval ring measuring 28 feet by 19 feet, and Gowlane North at 31 feet, unusual for the paired external stones forming a double portal.

A distinguishing feature of many of the stone circles of Co. Cork is the presence of a horizontal axial stone, erstwhile referred to as a ‘recumbent stone’, which is aligned with two dominant portal stones placed directly opposite. This characteristic has led to a parallel being drawn with the axial stone circles of Aberdeen in Scotland, though there the arrangement of the stones is somewhat different. The occurrence of the axial stone has provided a strong argument in favour of the theory that these structures were erected for an astronomical purpose. Other discoveries have strengthened this notion. Inside Kealkil circle near Bantry, excavators found channels in the ground crossing at right angles, marks which were interpreted as depressions made by timbers which could have supported a vertical sighting post.

Attempts to establish precise celestial alignments for these monuments tend to be inconclusive, not because none could be discovered, but because those that were could not be shown to be the result of intentional planning. The probability of fortuitous alignments occurring is high, and while some circles revealed several possibilities, others produced none. That is not to say that orientation played no part in the layout of these rings: on the contrary, it is noteworthy that the axial stone circles of Munster are nearly always aligned north-east/south-west, that is, with the portal stones facing sunrise and the axial stone facing sunset. But there is sufficient deviation from one circle to another to suggest that precise alignment was not required and that orientation was more likely to be connected with ritual than with scientific study.

The few stone circles that have been excavated in Ireland produced little firm dating evidence, with the exception of The Lios, a large and thoroughly investigated monument in Co. Limerick, the ample finds from which enabled archaeologists to assign it with a fair degree of certainty to the Early Bronze Age. A similar date seems likely for Beaghmore, though there the evidence is somewhat diffused by the fact that it is superimposed on an earlier, Neolithic settlement site.

A clue to the possible uses of stone circles might be sought in folklore. The seven stones of Lissyviggeen are explained in an old legend as the children of two giants (represented by a pair of tall outliers), all of whom were turned to stone as they danced. The theme of ossified dancers recurs in connection with other stone circles, both in Ireland and Britain, and since folklore often preserves elements of fact, one might conclude that dancing in celebration of pastoral festivals figured in the rites practised at these monuments, though this can only be part of the answer. In the end the mystery remains, tantalisingly locked forever in the stones themselves and in the lost culture of the people who built them.

The most ubiquitous of all prehistoric monuments is the standing stone, called *gallán*, or *dallán* in Irish. They are so numerous in the countryside that they defy counting, though some are considered important enough to be included on Ordnance Survey maps. Few have been excavated and dating evidence is scant. While many, perhaps even the majority, may be assigned to the Bronze Age, their possible uses are so varied that their erection must have extended over a very long time. There can be little doubt that some had sacred significance: a number are found as free-standing pillars in the chambers of passage tombs, thus tracing their origins as far back as the Neolithic; and the legendary *Crom Cruaich*, a standing stone said to have been overthrown by St Patrick, was an object of pagan worship. Others may have been set up as memorials – many certainly mark Bronze Age burials – and to define territorial boundaries and routeways, and some seem to have anthropomorphic personalities. Male and female characteristics have been attributed to pairs of standing stones whose respective shapes appear to support this interpretation. One such duo near the village of Saggart, Co. Dublin, is known as Adam and Eve.

The curious 'hole stones' comprise a small group of perhaps no more than a few dozen, whose wide distribution and onetime adoption as healing stones and for other obscure practices makes them of special interest. Similar customs are found associated with 'capped' standing stones, those with a small boulder set on top: St Olan's Stone at Aghabolloge in Co. Cork, Edenmore in Co. Down and The White Wife near Portrush are good documented examples. The two last named were periodically whitewashed in observance of local traditions which may once have been widespread, and possibly of considerable antiquity.

The transition from prehistory to early Christian period saw the appearance of Ogham script, an early form of writing that has been described as 'Ireland's first venture into literacy', employing a series of strokes, singly or in groups, inscribed across or on either side of a stem line. Here was another use for the serviceable standing stone, along whose vertical edge the characters could be cut. Several hundred Ogham stones have been recorded, overwhelmingly in the southern half of the country. Most decipherable inscriptions are commemorative, usually relating to individuals and their antecedents.

Many pre-existing standing stones were made acceptable to the Christian religion by carving simple crosses on them. From such tentative beginnings the early cross-slabs evolved, and ultimately the tall freestanding High Crosses which represent the supreme artistic achievement of the Celtic Church. They may seem an unlikely progeny of the pagan cult of great stones, but as Estyn Evans concluded, 'In a sense the High Crosses are the culminating expression of a reverence for the megalithic in the Atlantic zone of the British Isles'.

Over the centuries ancient sites acquired names and associations to fit the timeframe of legends and folklore, and many of the old sacred locations were again venerated, now as places of pilgrimage whose patterns and festive gatherings were ostensibly Christian, but whose origins lay in a shadowy pagan past.

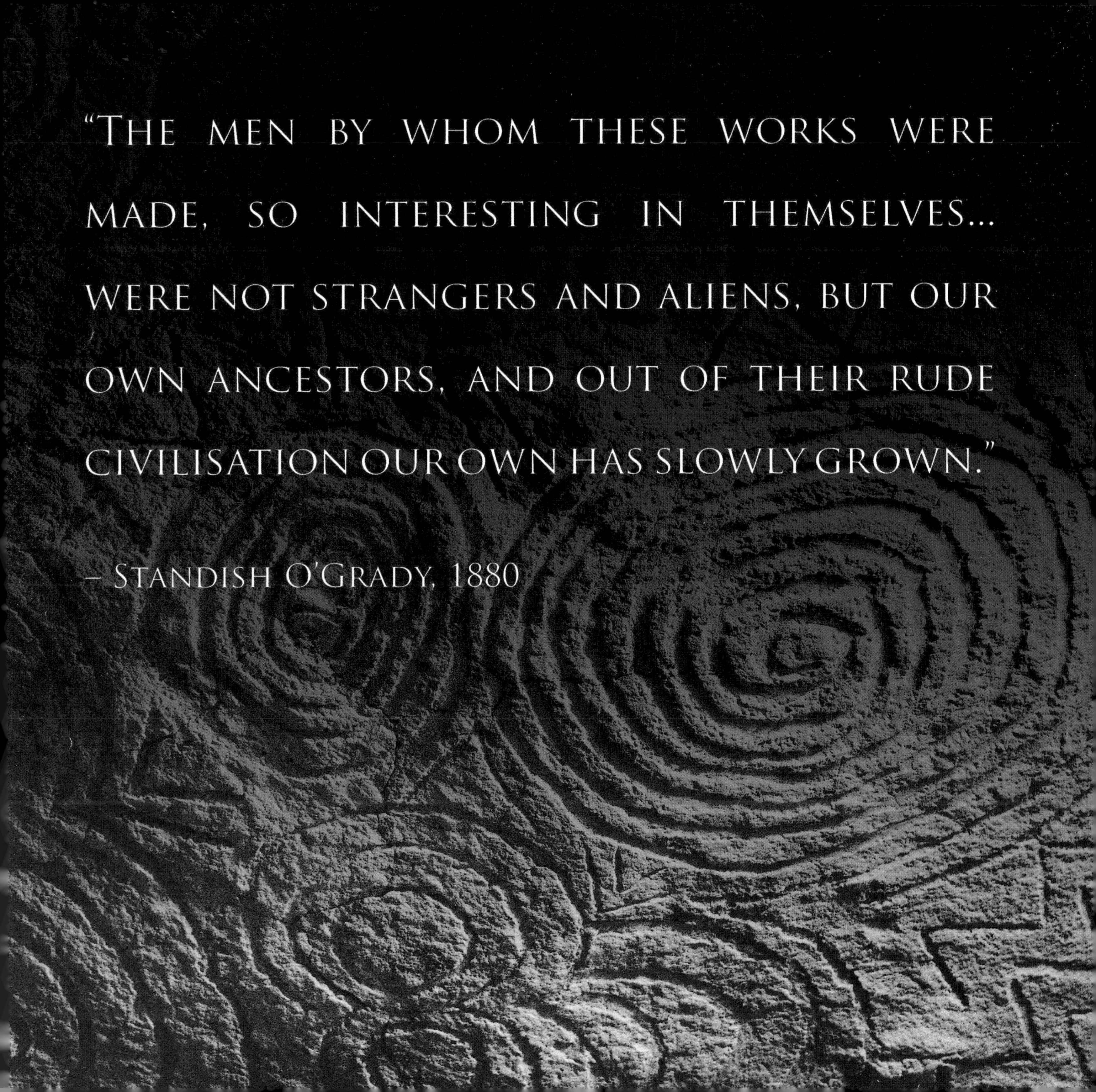

"The men by whom these works were made, so interesting in themselves... were not strangers and aliens, but our own ancestors, and out of their rude civilisation our own has slowly grown."

– Standish O'Grady, 1880

BALLYMACDERMOT

COUNTY ARMAGH

The siting of this very fine example of a single court tomb, at a height of 600 feet on the south side of Ballymacdermot Mountain some 2 miles south-west of Newry, is spectacular, with uninterrupted views across the Meigh plain to the great sweep of hills known as the Ring of Gullion. Yet the tomb has its back turned on this inspiring scenery, with the entrance facing northward between the 'horns' of the forecourt. Perhaps the view was intended for the benefit of those who would have gathered in the court to witness the funerary rites.

This must have been a difficult location for the builders who had to contend not only with the slope of the hill but also, as excavation showed, to clear the ground of undergrowth, and possibly trees, before construction could begin. The tapered cairn, 90 feet long, is well defined and survives to the height of the gallery walls. Of the three chambers, the middle one is the most substantial, with impressively tall entrance jambs and massive sidestones which still support some of the slipped roof corbels. The first chamber is by comparison small and narrow with low portals and had apparently served as an antechamber, since no evidence of burials was found. The rear chamber was the only one which contained undisturbed material and from it cremated bones and Neolithic pottery fragments were recovered. It is interesting that the tallest orthostats of the court occur at the eastern extremity, rather than following the more usual practice of placing them adjacent to the gallery entrance for emphasis.

While many megaliths have been damaged by vandalism, and removal of stone for building, only Ballymacdermot can claim collision with an American army tank. The incident occurred during Wartime manoeuvres in 1942, resulting in several façade stones being shorn off at ground level. After excavation in 1962, the broken portions were reunited with their bases and this repair work can be seen on the outer stones on the east side of the court.

Top: Forecourt from north-west

Bottom Right: Gallery entrance and first chamber

Bottom Left: Interior of middle chamber, looking north

KEMPE STONES

COUNTY DOWN

A well-known, though not all that easy to find local landmark, (it was, but is no longer signposted) the Kempe Stones are an excellent example of a portal tomb or dolmen, 1½ miles east of Dundonald village. It is best approached from Greengraves road leading south off the dual carriageway, then over a stile into a field. The megalith is incorporated in a boundary fence and overgrown with gorse, but close inspection is possible and worthwhile as it exhibits very clearly the classic structural features of the type, and is one of the most intact in the county. A bulky basalt capstone, 8 feet long and 7 feet wide, projects over the entrance and rests at the back on a secondary flat capstone. The single chamber, now a repository for field stones, is approximately square in plan and formed by five orthostats

Below: The Kempe Stones, from south

including the matched and pointed portal stones, 5 feet high and facing east. Between them is a sillstone rising to half their height. The tomb was contained in a long cairn some of which survives, and several large boulders half-buried in the field below presumably came from the kerb.

The old name of Greengraves townland was *Baile Chloch Togala*, 'townland of the raised stone', and was still in use in the eighteenth century. At what time the dolmen became known as the Kempe Stones is uncertain: *kempe* is an archaic Anglo-Saxon word signifying a warrior or champion.

PUNCHESTOWN (bottom left)

COUNTY KILDARE

This is the best known of a distinctive group of granite 'long stones' in the county, a tall, slender monolith conspicuous by the roadside in the townland of Punchestown Great (of racecourse fame), a little over 2 miles north-east of Naas. It fell from its tilted position in 1931 and lay until 1934 when it was re-erected in its former socket. Excavations carried out at the time uncovered an empty Bronze Age cist alongside the base, implying that its purpose was commemorative. The overall length of the prostrate stone was 23 feet and its weight was recorded at just over 9 tons. It now stands 19 feet high and is the tallest pillarstone in Ireland; the previous claimant to the title (by a margin of 9 inches), Bawnatemple in Co. Cork, crashed to the ground in 1985. Almost as impressive is the 14-feet high Long Stone of Craddockstown West, less than ½ mile east of here.

KILLADANGAN

COUNTY MAYO

Lying in the shadow of Croagh Patrick, Ireland's holy mountain, 4 miles west-south-west of Westport, to the north (sea side) of the road to Louisburgh, this interesting if scarcely conspicuous group of megaliths comprises three individual standing stones, a stone pair, remains of one and possibly two stone circles and a four-stone alignment. The site, called in Irish *Gortabrund*, is a salt marsh bordering on Clew Bay and is permanently waterlogged in places, with several of the stones rising picturesquely from dark peaty pools. Observations by members of Mayo Archaeological Society have shown that the alignment is orientated towards a V-shaped gap in the east shoulder of Croagh Patrick, through which the sun sinks on 21 December, the mid-winter solstice. A Bronze Age date seems likely for this group of monuments. That it may have been a more complex ceremonial site than the surviving evidence suggests is indicated by the first Ordnance Survey in the 1830s, which recorded more extensive remains here.

Above: Killadangan alignment

Right: Standing stones rise out of the salt marsh at the edge of Clew Bay

LOUGH MONEY

County Down

Contrary to appearances, this small 'dolmen' is probably a remnant of a more extensive galleried tomb whose stones have been pillaged. It sits picturesquely on a hill crest east of the junction of Lough Money and Carrownacaw roads, ¾ mile south-by-east of Raholp. A pair of long sidestones support an overhanging capstone measuring 10 by 5 feet. The overall height of the chamber is 5½ feet. There is no trace of a cairn to indicate to what class of tomb this belonged.

This is a very pleasant location ringed by little hills and stone-walled fields, with glimpses of Strangford Lough to the north. When visiting this megalith it is worthwhile continuing on Carrownacaw road for about ⅓ mile to arrive at the 'Long Stone', a slender monolith nearly 10 feet tall. It has acquired a pronounced lean, and to prevent its collapse is now tethered by a steel cable to a convenient tree.

CLONLUM

COUNTY ARMAGH

Situated in a field to the east of a tree-lined country road below Slieve Gullion, ½ mile west-north-west of the village of Meigh, this late Neolithic tomb preserves much of its cairn, 35 feet in diameter and 4 feet high. Partly buried at the centre is a dolmen with a large capstone, now displaced and split in two, which when intact would have measured 9 by 5½ feet. The rectangular chamber is closed at each end and has flanking portal stones 7 feet tall at the west: one of these is fallen which may have caused the capstone to collapse. Several mature larch trees which grew on the cairn last century have been removed because of the damage their roots were inflicting. Excavation of the tomb in 1934 was disappointing in finds. As so often turns out to be the case, treasure-seekers had been there before. Clonlum may represent a transition from the truly megalithic to less elaborate forms of tomb building, ultimately the box-like cists of the Bronze Age and early Iron Age, whose economical features are perhaps recognisable here in the construction of the chamber.

Above: The broken capstone lies over the open chamber.

AGHNACLIFF

COUNTY LONGFORD

There are few dolmens in this part of the country and this is an especially interesting, not to say extraordinary example. It can be reached by crossing several fields behind Aghnacliff church, or more directly by continuing south for a short distance past the village, where a signed lane to the east of the road provides access. The megalith stands near the bottom of a sloping field not far from a small stream. It is an astonishing sight. One of the portal stones is missing, leaving the bulky 10-feet long capstone supported at the front by a single upright, and at the back by a smaller secondary capstone covering the chamber. It has, however, somehow managed to maintain this gravity-defying equilibrium for a very long time and presumably will continue to do so for the foreseeable future. The surviving portal stone has a small cross inscribed on it, perhaps a legacy of Penal times when mass was celebrated in secret, often with a megalithic tomb as a place of assembly.

BOHONAGH

COUNTY CORK

Above: Bohonagh. The tall portal stones in the foreground frame the recumbent, or axial stone, at the far side of the circle.

An incomplete but nonetheless very fine example of a recumbent stone circle of West Munster type, situated on a low hill within sight of the coast, 1½ miles east of Ross Carbery. Its diameter of 30 feet is typical of several in the area including nearby Drombeg and Reanascreena South. The tapered portal stones are set radially on an east-west axis with the recumbent stone opposite, providing an alignment on the equinoctial sunset. They are among the tallest of any Irish open circle, the larger of the pair standing almost 8 feet above ground.

Excavation in 1959 established that the circle had thirteen stones, of which six remained upright, three lay fallen and four were missing. The fallen stones were re-erected in their original sockets using a system of timber levers. As at Drombeg, a small pit at the centre of the circle was found to contain cremated remains, possibly placed there as a ritual dedication of the monument. To the east of the circle is a boulder dolmen with a cup-marked capstone. Both megaliths, and possibly also traces of a timber hut site discovered nearby, belong in the Bronze Age.

BEENALAGHT

County Cork

This superb alignment of massive stones is known as *An Seisear* ('The Six'), and although one of its number is fallen this is still one of the best megalithic rows in the county. It occupies a level site up on Reanthesure, at the foot of Bweengduff Mountain, 8½ miles south-west of Mallow, and is visible at a distance of about 500 yards to the west of the Bweeng-Coachford road. It has been observed that alignment stones are sometimes graded in one direction according to height, but no general rule applies to all. Here the tallest stones are placed at the extremities of the row with the shortest in the middle. Their heights range from 6 to over 9 feet, orientated north-east/south-west over a distance of 36 feet. The site has not been excavated – these structures are unlikely to yield artifacts or firm dating evidence – but it fits into the broad timeframe of Bronze Age ritual monuments that includes most stone circles. Alignments tend to be sited in prominent places in the landscape, presumably as part of their function, but the fine views they once commanded are today often obscured by state forestry plantations.

MAGHERAGHANRUSH

COUNTY SLIGO

Leacht con Mhic Ruis is a large and relatively well-preserved example of a centre court tomb 4 miles east of Sligo town. It is beautifully sited on a prominent limestone ridge overlooking a panorama of countryside and coast – unfortunately screened from view by the recent planting of conifer trees around the megalith. The overall length of the monument is about 100 feet, comprising a long, somewhat oval-shaped court with twin galleries opening off its east end and a single gallery at the west, each divided into two chambers. The court is entered through a gap mid-way along its south side.

Until a century or so ago all three galleries retained their lintel stones across the entrance jambs, but now only that on the north-east survives, split in two and leaning precariously inward. On the hill below are other early remains that include a wrecked wedge tomb and a stone-built ring-fort with a roofless souterrain at its centre.

Above: Magheraghanrush. Interior of western gallery, looking east towards court

Above: Entrance to western gallery at Magheraghanrush with prostrate slab in front

BEAGHMORE

COUNTY TYRONE

This extraordinary megalithic complex lies at the eastern margin of the Sperrin Mountains, 8½ miles west-north-west of Cookstown and just 2 miles from the Londonderry border. Completely buried in peat bog, it came to light in the early 1940s as the result of domestic turfcutting, and was taken into state care several years later. Beaghmore means 'great birches', and while the name itself may not be of great antiquity, it serves as an oblique reminder that these exposed uplands once nurtured a varied woodland before it was transformed by Neolithic farmers who cleared the trees and turned the land over to crop production.

The monuments uncovered comprise seven stone circles, ten alignments and twelve cairns. Six of the circles are grouped in pairs and all have associated alignments extending tangentially from them, usually with a cairn as a focal point. The solitary circle, E, is the largest here and is unusual in that its interior is densely studded with small stones – apparently there are 884 of them – known as the 'Dragon's Teeth'. The two south-westerly circles, F and G, are the smallest of the group and share a single alignment of low stones stretching for a distance of nearly 70 feet. Circle G is notable for a pair of large portal stones indicating an entrance at the south-east. Nearby is a small cairn with encircling fosse, a feature that suggests henge affinities. Several of the cairns covered cists containing cremated bone.

As with most of the circles found in mid-Ulster, the stones here are generally of small size, with one or two exceptions in circle E. Only the alignments can be fairly described as megalithic, some of their stones standing 4-5 feet in height. What little dating evidence there is places Beaghmore in the early Bronze Age. Excavation also revealed that it overlay a Neolithic cultivation site, and it has been suggested that the erection of these ritual monuments was in response to deteriorating soil fertility and the encroachment of peat. Eventually even the tallest stones were overwhelmed as bog growth accelerated in the first millennium BC, concealing them from sight until now. Further stones may be spotted to the east and south, and others occasionally come to light as a plot of land is reclaimed for building on; a three-stone row stands on the lawn of a house ½ mile away, evidence of just how extensive this complex site really is.

Above: Alignments and stone circles

Right: Plan of Beaghmore complex

Far Right: Circles F and G, and cairn with surrounding fosse

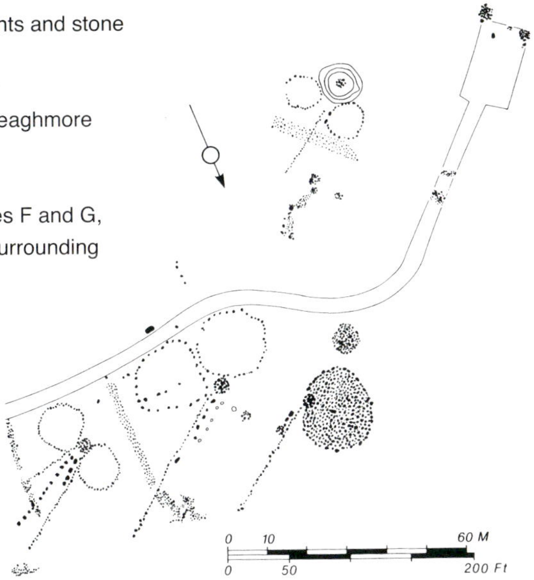

TIRNONY

COUNTY LONDONDERRY

A small but fairly impressive dolmen, and a good example of its class, situated at a corner on Tirnony road, which leads north from the road to Tirkane 1 mile north-west of Maghera. A rectangular chamber of five uprights opens east between a matched pair of portal stones 5 feet high, on which is perched a craggy capstone tilted at a jaunty angle like a beret worn on the side of the head. It is supported mainly by the sloping tops of the portal stones and retained in position by a massive sidestone. A roofstone is missing from the back of the chamber allowing its interior to be clearly seen.

Flanking the north portal is a free-standing orthostat, 4 feet tall, which appears to be a remnant of a façade, thus providing evidence of a link between portal and court tombs.

PADDOCK

COUNTY LOUTH

Situated just under 1 mile north-east of the celebrated monastic site of Monasterboice, which is 5 miles north-west of Drogheda, 'Calliagh Birra's House' is a little known and heavily overgrown

wedge tomb now incorporated in, and confused by, a field bank. In 1866, when the above drawing was made, the megalith was described as 'in a very good state of preservation'. Standing a little over 4 feet high, the 15-feet long gallery is composed of five stones on each side and roofed with four large flat slabs. The entrance, which unusually for a wedge tomb faces east, is partly destroyed. A curious feature is a series of 'stunted buttresses' set at right angles to the south side of the gallery: they may have linked the customary double-walling found in this class of tomb, but which in this example has been almost completely removed.

Above: Wedge tomb at Paddock, north side of gallery

LONGSTONE RATH

County Kildare

The name of this complex monument, on a prominent hill in the private demesne of Furness House 3 miles east-north-east of Naas, is misleading, for although it resembles a large domestic rath it is in fact a Bronze Age ceremonial site or sanctuary. A place of potent atmosphere, even on a sunlit afternoon, it consists of a tree-grown earthen bank up to 9 feet high with entrance gaps on the east and west, enclosing a circular area 190 feet in diameter and surrounded by an external fosse. Excavation in 1912 uncovered evidence that an intense fire had burned over a large part of the interior and this

area had later been covered with a mound of earth and boulders. At the centre of the enclosure stands a 17½-feet tall pillarstone of Wicklow granite, its base held in a rock-cut socket. Its slender form is comparable to others of the Kildare group of monoliths and it comes closest to Punchestown in size and appearance, though with an estimated weight of 12 tons it ranks as the heavier. Adjoining it is a long cist which contained cremated remains, pottery sherds and items of ornament. The excavation report noted that 'One of the trees – a Hawthorn – still preserves spiritual values in local tradition. The place, it appears, is visited by girls desiring husbands, who stick a pin in the back of the tree as a reminder of their visit, or sometimes tie on a rag'. The custom of depositing personal mementos here continued through much of last century and may not be totally extinct even now.

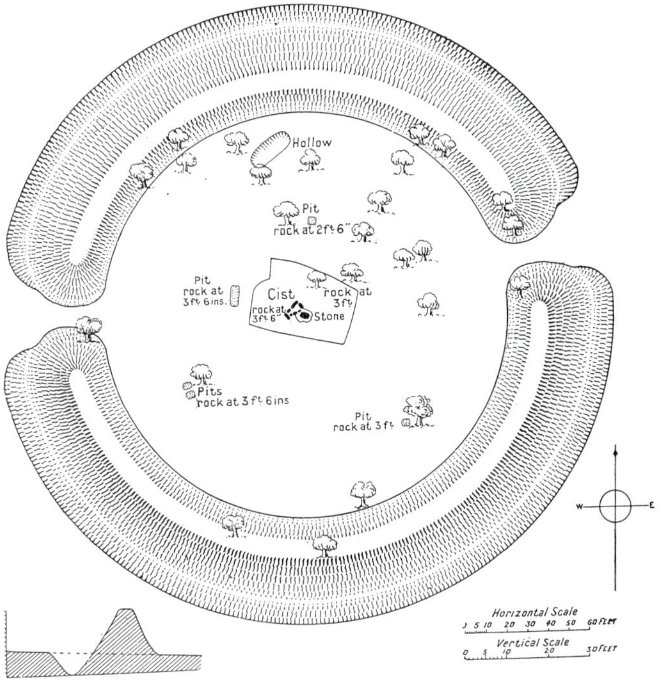

Above: Pillarstone at centre of enclosure

Right: Plan of earthwork

GOWARD

COUNTY DOWN

Standing amid gently undulating countryside bordering the Mourne Mountains, this famous dolmen (not to be confused with Goward Court Tomb which is described on *page 119*) is known variously as 'The Cloghmore', 'Finn's Finger' and 'Pat Kearney's Big Stone' (after the occupant of an adjacent cottage in the early 1900s who took a proprietorial interest in the monument). It is one of the largest and most remarkable megaliths in the county and also one of the more accessible, at the end of a byroad leading south from the Hilltown to Castlewellan road, 2½ miles northeast of the former. The great capstone, 13 feet long and estimated to weigh 40-50 tons, has slew sideways and now overhangs the chamber on the north, tilted to a height of 14 feet above ground. The exposed chamber is rectangular in plan, 9 feet long and unsegmented, with side walls 3 feet high and a tall closing slab at the entrance, which faces east. A horizontal slab at the back of the chamber may be a secondary capstone, if it is not a collapsed backstone. Flanking stones at the entrance suggest that there may have been a curved façade in the manner of court tombs, from which portal tombs as a class are thought to have evolved. All the structural stones are granite.

Like many megaliths, Goward has not escaped human interference. In 1834 *The Dublin Penny Journal* reported that 'it is now converted into a sty for pigs', and goes on to describe an

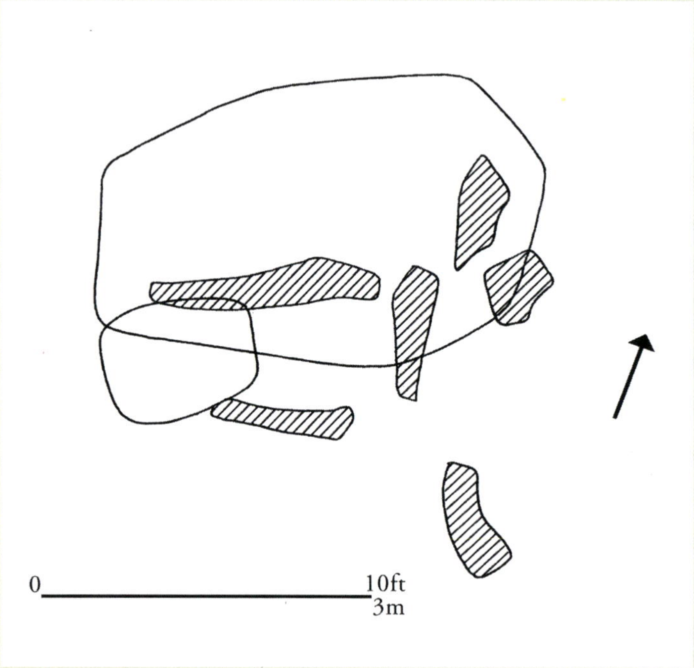

urn found in the chamber 'with beautiful figures cut on it, and likewise a representation of the sun and moon'. It is said that stones appropriated from the cairn surrounding the dolmen were used to build Pat Kearney's cottage, which has crumbled away to the moss-covered boulders lying nearby. Only the Cloghmore remains, a silent and immutable witness to the passing centuries.

Top: Plan of chamber showing position of displaced capstone

Bottom: The megalith at dusk

KILTIERNAN

COUNTY DUBLIN

This magnificent portal tomb is one of several megaliths in the Dublin area illustrated by Gabriel Beranger, an antiquarian artist working in Ireland in the latter half of the eighteenth century. Beranger clearly recognised the importance of recording these ancient remains which were often endangered, and which in some instances have since disappeared. Fortunately this great dolmen has survived and remains much as he saw it over two centuries ago. Beranger often introduced human figures into his watercolours to convey a sense of scale, and here he shows two surveyors at work, dwarfed by the huge capstone they are engaged in measuring. The person supervising this activity is in all probability Beranger, who sometimes included himself in his compositions.

The picture may have been the inspiration for Borlase's description of this monument as 'a sphinx-like monster, advancing out of a rocky hill on some half dozen short and rickety legs'. It is situated among boulder-strewn fields 1 mile south-south-east of Stepaside, which is about 7 miles south-east of Dublin. Permission to visit the site may be refused due to a recent dispute over public access.

The plan of the chamber is confused, but measures some 15 feet in length, unusually large for a portal tomb, and it may have been built thus to accommodate the length of the capstone, which at 22 feet is among the largest of its kind. It is possible that this massive stone was already at hand for the builders to make use of: a rocky ledge rising behind the tomb is a likely place from which it could

which over time have been pushed askew by its unrelenting weight, estimated at 40 tons. Remedial work to stabilise the structure in 1956 recovered several artifacts from the chamber including coarse decorated pottery. Kiltiernan probably belongs, like its fellow dolmens in the district, to the late Neolithic period, 2500-2000 BC.

Top: Kiltiernan dolmen as it appears today, scarcely changed from Beranger's illustration of 1776

CLOCHAFARMORE

COUNTY LOUTH

'So stood Cúchulainn, even in death's pangs a terror to his enemies and the bulwark of his nation'

The name Clochafarmore is a corruption by the 1834 Ordnance Survey of *Cloch an Fhir Mhoir*, meaning 'the Stone of the Great Man'. According to oral tradition still strong here, it was to this hoary pillarstone that the mortally wounded hero Cúchulainn bound himself and stood, sword in hand, to face the advancing army of Queen Maeve of Connacht. The mighty Ulster warrior knew that as long as his enemies believed he was still alive they would not dare to approach, so great was their awe of him. The standoff held for a while, until Mór-Rioghain, the goddess of battle, took the form of a raven and settled on his shoulder, and it at last became evident that he had succumbed.

Travelling from Dundalk in the direction of the county town of Louth, the Clochafarmore can be seen on rising ground south of the road in Rathiddy, 1 mile east of Knockbridge. Standing over 9 feet high and leaning, it looks like a gnarled and ancient tree trunk, scarred by centuries of weathering and encrusted with lichen, the lower part burnished by cattle rubbing against it. A deep split runs from top to bottom, hinting at powerful stresses at work long ago. Altogether a remarkable stone, a still potent symbol of defiance in the face of overwhelming odds.

It was the Celtic revivalist Standish O'Grady who put literary flesh on the Cúchulainn legend and established him as an iconic figure in the national psyche. In the wake of the 1916 Easter Rising in Dublin, the erstwhile defender of Ulster's borderlands became an unlikely metaphor for the insurgents bold but ill-fated stand at the General Post Office, wherein Oliver Sheppard's commemorative statue, *The Death of Cúchulainn*, presides over the daily business of selling stamps and postal orders.

DUNLOE

County Kerry

Seven ogham stones have been re-erected as a roadside group in the grounds of Dunloe castle, 6 miles west of Killarney. All but one were unearthed from a souterrain at Coolmagort in the nineteenth century. The largest stands 8 feet high and is supported on a reinforced backing. Ogham stones were often appropriated for use as roofing slabs in souterrains in the early Christian period because of their convenient size and shape. Long protection from exposure has ensured that the Dunloe examples are unusually well preserved, with crisp inscriptions reading vertically upwards from the bottom of the stone. One has been Christianised by the addition of a cross. The fact that seven were built into one souterrain is an indication of just how numerous these monoliths must have been at one time – another souterrain at Drumlohan in Co. Waterford contained no fewer than ten. The use of ogham script spanned a period of roughly 500 years from about 300 AD.

A mutilated but very impressive stone circle crowning an exposed hilltop 2 miles south of Raphoe. The site, which commands extensive views, takes its name from the Celtic pastoral festival of Beltaine, 1 May, and while it possibly did become the focus of this celebration, the monument belongs to a much earlier time. About sixty stones remain *in situ*, enclosing a ring with a diameter of 150 feet. Many more have evidently been removed or displaced. The ransacked interior is several feet higher than the ground outside and is littered with boulder debris. Some of the stones are exceptionally large, up to 8 feet in height, and many lean haphazardly outward under pressure from the raised interior. A shapely standing stone forms a solitary outlier 70 feet to the south-east. Possible astronomical alignments have been advanced for some of the circle stones: one, perhaps fortuitously, points to sunrise at or about Beltaine. This monument is difficult to classify because of its hybrid features. It may be the remains of a despoiled cairn, though no clear evidence of a chamber has been reported, and the stones resemble those of a ritual circle rather than a conventional kerb. There are some similarities with Ballynoe in Co. Down, where a burial mound or barrow is surrounded by a ring of massive standing stones.

Not all that easy to find in a vast featureless peat bog some 3 miles south-west of Dromore West, near the Owenykeevan river, lie the Great and Small Griddles of the Fianna (so named after the warrior elite of Celtic legend). The Griddles, one a court tomb, the other a wedge tomb, both in somewhat ruined state, stand several hundred yards apart and can be approached by turfcutters' paths through the bog. This comparatively remote location is of interest as one of the megalithic sites surveyed by the antiquarian artist Gabriel Beranger during his tour of Connacht in 1779, when he became hopelessly lost 'in this horrid wilderness'. Not far from here, in the same tract of bogland in Tawnatruffaun townland, is the altogether more impressive Giant's Griddle, a fairly well-preserved portal tomb.

Previous page: Outlying standing stone at Beltany on Tops Mountain

Bottom Left: Some of the sixty large orthostats of Beltany stone circle

Bottom Right: 'The Great Griddle' court tomb

CARROWMORE

County Sligo

'This remarkable series of ancient monuments, excepting the monuments of Carnac in Brittany, is, even in the present state of ruin, the largest assemblage of the kind hitherto discovered in the world.'

– G Petrie

When George Petrie of the Historical Commission attached to the Ordnance Survey visited Carrowmore in 1837 he was dismayed by what he found: 'The destruction going on daily is horrible', he reported, 'and if I did not work now it would be too late'. His words were prophetic. Damage caused by commercial gravel quarrying, vandalism by treasure seekers and general neglect by the authorities has reduced the number of monuments recorded by Petrie from around sixty (he estimated that there could have been as many as a hundred originally) to less than thirty today. As recently as 1983, Sligo County Council proposed siting a refuse dump in the area, a plan vigorously opposed by local people and influential outsiders, and, after a lengthy legal battle, overruled by the Supreme Court. Now vested in the Office of Public Works and provided with a small interpretative visitor centre, Carrowmore has belatedly been given the protection it so long deserved.

There is still much to see at this remarkable place 2 miles south-west of Sligo, containing the largest group of megaliths in Ireland, and a fair amount of time is required to explore it properly. The surviving monuments are distributed over several acres of Carrowmore and extend into adjoining townlands. At first sight these look like typical dolmen structures but are in fact small passage tombs stripped of their covering cairns, leaving the central chambers standing in isolation. Some are ringed by massive boulder kerbs, and sometimes the kerb itself is all that remains, resembling a ritual stone circle. The locally available materials used in building these tombs – mostly erratics deposited by the retreating ice sheets 10,000 years ago – clearly influenced their simple form. Unlike the sophisticated corbelling found in passage tombs elsewhere, they are roofed with a single large capstone in the manner of portal tombs, resulting in chambers whose internal height is determined by the supporting uprights.

Until recently it was believed that this group of monuments lacked the ornamentation of passage tombs in the east of the country. Apart from a stray example noted in a chamber at Cloverhill, some distance from the main concentration, no decorative motifs had been discovered; until in 1994 close examination of the capstone of the largest tomb, Listoghil (Petrie's No. 51), revealed faint but unmistakable curvilinear designs. It is perhaps significant that this tomb is sited in a central position to the others, whose entrances in many instances face inwards towards it.

The question of date is a vexed issue. It had long been assumed that these monuments belonged to a late phase of passage tomb building, but a series of excavations by a Swedish archaeologist, Goran Burenholt, appear to turn that hypothesis on its head, placing Carrowmore right at the beginning of the megalithic tradition in Ireland, indeed, long before the great tombs of the Boyne Valley. Even more controversial is his conclusion that at least one of the megaliths here was built, not by Neolithic farmers, but by their foraging Mesolithic predecessors.

Overlooking the necropolis, on the 1014-feet summit of Knocknarea, is the great stone cairn known as *Miosgan Meadhbha*, 200 feet wide at the base and piled up to over 30 feet high, celebrated in legend as the burial place of Queen Maeve of Connacht. It has never been excavated and no entrance has been found, but its siting and general appearance suggest that it too is a passage tomb, perhaps the spiritual and secular focus of the myriad sepulchres spread out below. Recent and ongoing excavation work around Knocknarea is providing evidence that this entire area is even more important archaeologically than previously recognised.

TAMNAHARRY

County Down

Of the many standing stones dotted around the Mourne Mountains, 'Cloghadda', 2 miles due south of Mayobridge, is one of the finest, and most secluded. Sited at an altitude of 800 feet between the summits of Craignamona and Slievecarnane, it is approached by a long uphill walk across heathery moorland, at the end of which the stone comes suddenly into view, looking like a giant thumb sticking out of the ground. The massive granite monolith stands

Above: Listoghil dolmen, focal monument of the Carrowmore complex

Right: Massive boulder kerbs surround many of the tombs at Carrowmore

Far Right: Denuded passage tomb chamber with Knocknarea in the background

nearly 9 feet high and is notable for the smooth hollow or 'shoulder' near the top which has the appearance of having been produced, or at least emphasised, by artificial means. The hillocks on either side afford lofty views across wide expanses of Co. Down countryside to the north and of Carlingford Lough and its backdrop of mountains away to the south.

Not far from Cloghadda is the even taller 'Long Stone of Mayo', rising from a broad base to a height of 9½ feet. One of the more accessible standing stones in the district, it is situated behind a farmyard on the west side of the Mayobridge to Rostrevor road, ½ mile south of the former and can be glimpsed, framed by trees, from the public road. For closer inspection, permission of the landowner should be sought.

Right: Kilmogue dolmen depicted in an engraving of 1809

Far Right: A comparable view of the megalith today

KILMOGUE

COUNTY KILKENNY

'A proof of the resources, if not the mathematical skill, of our ancestors, for with all the assistance of the improved machinery of the moderns, it is not possible that such ponderous masses could be raised now, and placed in similar positions, with such geometrical accuracy'

– Joseph T. Finegan, 1807

The Irish name of this spectacular dolmen is *Leac an Scail*, sometimes translated as 'the stone of the champion', or alternatively, 'the stone that casts a shadow'. Situated a little over ½ mile from Harristown crossroads, 7 miles east-north-east of Carrick-on-Suir, it is partly hidden by rampant hedges in a low-lying corner of a field next to a farmyard. A small stream flows nearby. This is the tallest portal tomb in the country, towering to a height of 15 feet at the front of the steeply angled capstone, whose lower end rests on a horizontal roofstone at the back of the chamber. The majestic portal stones stand 12 feet high and have a tall doorstone between them to close the entrance. Loose material about the base of the tomb shows that it was contained in a cairn of earth and stones, but it is unlikely to have been completely covered over.

TOBERNAVEEN

County Sligo

Heavily overgrown and difficult to reach – it is situated in a virtual swamp – this well-documented stone, 2 miles south-west of Sligo, lives up to its name, *Clocha Breca* ('Speckled Stone'), so called from its mottled surface, now overgrown with ivy and other vegetation. The massive limestone slab, 9 feet tall and nearly 10 feet wide, is pierced by a rectangular aperture offset to one side near the base. In earlier times the stone was venerated for its reputed healing powers, and sick children were passed through the 3 by 2 feet hole in expectation of a cure. The origin of this curious stone is unknown: it may have come from a megalithic tomb and could have been a closing slab with 'porthole entrance', a feature found in a small number of court tombs.

THE MASONBROOK RING

County Galway

The Masonbrook Ring, or 'The Seven Monuments', stands in the townland of Moanmore East nearly 2 miles south-east of Loughrea and immediately south of the road to Tynagh. A curious and anomalous monument, it consists of a circular earthen bank 70 feet in diameter and 3 feet high, on top of which, spaced at intervals of 25 feet or thereabouts, are seven standing stones set radially. They average 4½ feet in height, and two have recently fallen. A single gap in the bank forms an entrance. A small grass-grown cairn at the centre has been identified as an old Ordnance Survey marker and has no connection with the earthwork.

This atypical monument is difficult to classify, but could perhaps be described as an embanked stone circle, possibly in the

Above: The Dolmen of the Four Maols

circle-henge tradition, though it does not have a fosse and the placing of the stones on rim of the bank is unusual. Its authenticity has been called into question because some of the stones are known to have been re-erected from their fallen position in the nineteenth century. However, given that this area has a number of early earthworks and at least one megalithic tomb, it is reasonable to assume that The Ring is also a genuine antiquity, even if it has suffered from interference.

BALLINA

County Mayo

About ½ mile south-west of this lively market town, on Piper's hill with a view of the River Moy to the east, is this neat megalithic chamber which may be a portal tomb, or perhaps the remains of a small passage tomb. In size and appearance it recalls 'The Druid's Altar' at Islandmagee in Co. Antrim. A hexagonal capstone, 9 by 7 feet, rests horizontally on three chamber uprights; a fourth stone lies close by and may also have formed part of the chamber, which is orientated north-south.

In 1838 the antiquarian John O'Donovan identified this megalith as 'The Dolmen of the Four Maols', and the name has since become part of folklore. The tale concerns four foster-brothers

Bishop Cellach in the early Christian period. This would of course have post-dated the tomb by several thousand years, which in itself need not rule out some sort of connection – if the episode did indeed occur and was not merely a colourful invention.

REASK

COUNTY KERRY

Prehistoric standing stones are often found at early monastic sites where they were given a new lease of life by having crosses inscribed on them to disguise their pagan origins, a device which marked the beginnings of Irish ecclesiastical art. Sometimes the results of this fusion of cultures could be stunningly beautiful, as conveyed by the Reask cross-pillar, 1 mile east of Ballyferriter in the Dingle peninsula. The influence of late La Tène decoration is implicit in the flowing spiral design which so confidently exploits the natural facets of the stone. Although by no means all Christian cross-pillars started out as pre-existing standing stones, very many probably did, so numerous were the latter throughout the landscape. It was from rough and ready monoliths such as these that the shaped cross-slabs evolved, and in turn the fully developed High crosses whose richly sculptured scenes from the scriptures are among the greatest treasures of the Celtic church.

KILCLOONEY MORE

COUNTY DONEGAL

Two portal tombs, the little and large of Irish dolmens, stand at opposite ends of a long cairn, the larger one looming conspicuous on the skyline to the east of the Narin road, 4 miles north-north-east of Ardara. It is a truly remarkable structure, not only on account of its size and poise, but also for the ever changing profile it presents from different viewpoints: 'a prehistoric study in aerodynamics'; 'a great hat on legs'; 'a flying saucer landed in the bog'; 'a giant bird poised for flight' – these are some of the resemblances inspired by its intriguing form.

A magnificent granite capstone, broadly triangular in shape and measuring 19 feet across at its widest point, oversails the 6-feet high portal stones at the chamber entrance on the east. Its lower end rests on a 'chocking stone' which lifts it clear of the backstone of the chamber. The smaller dolmen at the west end of the cairn is partly collapsed and is crossed by a field wall, but still has its capstone in position over the rectangular chamber of two sidestones and a backstone. It also faces east and like the larger tomb, has a low sill between the portal stones, one of which is fallen. Some fragments of Neolithic pottery were the only finds from the site.

GORTAVERN

COUNTY DONEGAL

Sited in boggy pasture in the Burnside river valley, slightly less than 1 mile south of Carrowkeel and ¼ mile east of the road to Rathmelton, 'Dermot and Grania's Bed' is one of the county's lesser known megaliths, a somewhat disturbed but largely complete portal tomb. Two tall uprights at the entrance and a low backstone support a steeply angled capstone with a length of 12 feet, now slipped from its original position over the chamber, one of whose sidestones is fallen. Nonetheless, this remains a fine example of its class. Several cupmarks have been noted on top of the capstone.

POULNABRONE

County Clare

The stark but beautiful landscape of The Burren in north-west Clare is famed both for its unique flora and for a remarkable concentration of prehistoric remains, notably wedge tombs of a distinctive local type, and more particularly for this celebrated portal tomb which in the minds of many has become an icon of megalithic Ireland. It rises from an expanse of grey limestone pavement, 5 miles south of Ballyvaghan, its dramatic profile instantly recognisable against the sky, with a splendid 12-feet long tabular capstone soaring out over the slender portal stones. It has been aptly described as resembling a house of cards, and like one it came close to tumbling down some years ago when a severe crack was discovered in one of the portal stones, necessitating its temporary removal for repair. This provided an opportunity to carry out a scientific excavation of the chamber, with rewarding results, adding much to the understanding of the treatment of the dead for collective burial in these tombs.

DOONFEENY (right)

COUNTY MAYO

Commanding a fine vista of cliffed headlands, this ancient enclosure 2 miles north-west of Ballycastle is notable for the magnificent pillarstone it contains. Standing fully 17 feet high it ranks among the three or four tallest in the country, yet is not well known outside the district. It is exceptionally uniform along its length and slightly curved, though to a lesser degree than indicated by Westropp's sketch. Near the base are two simple inscribed crosses, the lower one embellished with stylised bird motifs. The odd placing of the carving so close to the base suggests it was executed *in situ*, and was, as Westropp concluded, 'an afterthought...it may be by some early missionary, to placate his converts to the faith, who still reverenced this ancient memorial'. In this way it was possible for pagan standing stones to be reconciled with Christian beliefs, and their occurrence at monastic sites is not uncommon.

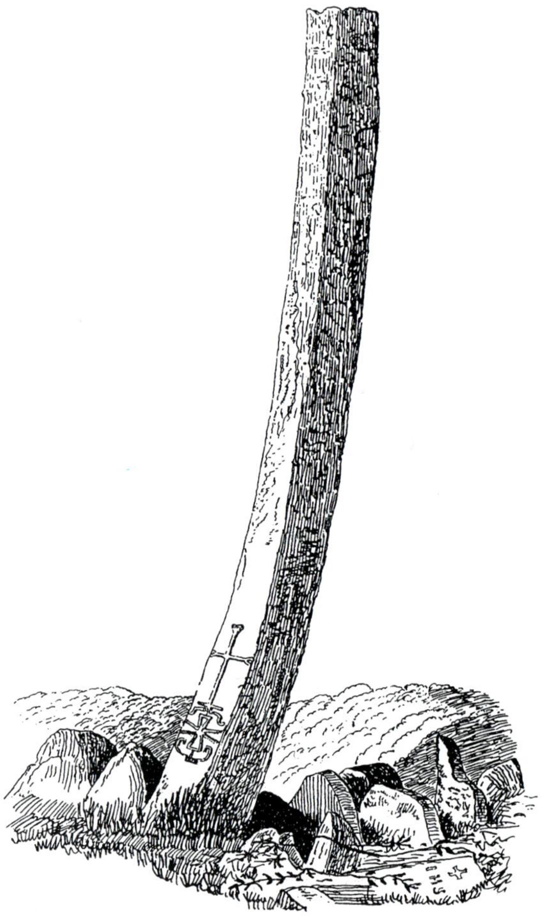

AUDLEYSTOWN

COUNTY DOWN

The main feature of interest of this dual-court tomb is its well-preserved cairn, the long and remarkably straight sides of which are retained by excellent dry-walling instead of the more usual orthostatic kerb. The pronounced wedge shape of the cairn is also noteworthy, with its widest end facing south-west. It is situated almost 2 miles west-north-west of Strangford village, close to the shore of the lough and about 1 mile west-south-west of Audley's castle.

As with many similar monuments in state care its presentation is not enhanced by the ugly protective wire fence surrounding it; but the structural layout of this type of megalithic tomb is here well displayed thanks to restoration work carried out following excavation in 1952. A shallow curved forecourt at each end of the cairn gives access to a roofless gallery of four chambers with segmenting jambs. The twin galleries are set back to back on a north-east/south-west axis, and some of the corbels which carried the roof slabs are still to be seen. A total of thirty-four burials, both inhumed and cremated, were distributed equally between the two galleries. A variety of Neolithic pottery and flint tools were also recovered.

Top Right: Sidestone and jambs in northern gallery

Bottom Left: Orthostats demarcating south-west forecourt

Bottom Right: East view of the cairn showing dry-walling revetment

DOAGH

COUNTY ANTRIM

A well-known and adequately signed monument, this shapely Hole Stone crowns a steep-sided rocky knoll 1½ miles north-west of the village of Doagh, to the east of a byroad leading north from the road to Kells. The outcrop on which it stands is heavily gorse-grown and the stone is only clearly visible from the top, which affords a 360 degree view of the surrounding countryside. The Hole Stone is a 5-feet high whinstone slab, 10 inches thick, tapering from a broad base to a blunt point offset to one side. It is pierced by a well-worn circular hole 3½ inches in diameter, widening out countersunk fashion on each side, and evidently produced by artificial means. It was formerly the custom for engaged couples to affirm their vows by clasping hands through this opening, whence its one-time sobriquet 'the love stone'.

The origin of the megalith is unknown, but it is possibly a relic of the Bronze Age and could have come from a destroyed tomb. In 1833 *The Dublin Penny Journal* printed a woodcut of the stone along with an account of troth-plighting commonly practised here; and Wood-Martin, writing in 1902, states that 'marriage contracts are still ratified at this spot as country couples go there to signify their betrothal clasping hands through the hole'. It is noted that the aperture is too small to permit the average size man's hand to pass through, so presumably it was the prerogative of the bride-to-be to offer hers. A hole stone on the island of Cape Clear in Co. Cork bears a striking resemblance to the Doagh monument and is known as *Cloch na nCealluna*, 'the promising stone'. As a class hole stones are not particularly numerous, with only a few dozen examples recorded countrywide. Most are associated with long-standing folk customs of various kinds, often centred on healing and fertility rites, some of whose origins may date back to prehistoric times.

TOOME

COUNTY DONEGAL

This neglected megalith lies near the northern end of Toome Lough below Trusklieve Mountain, about 10 miles south-by-east of Dunloe. At the west end of a long cairn (unfortunately littered with domestic rubbish when last seen) is 'Dermot and Grania's Bed', a collapsed dolmen immediately recognisable from the splendid pair of granite portal stones which taper gracefully to a height of 6 feet and have a doorstone set between them. The rectangular chamber is formed by two low sidestones and an endstone shaped like a gable. A slipped capstone lies inside the chamber. The tomb faces east into the body of the cairn, at whose opposite end some 30 feet distant are the remains of a second tomb, which is in an even more collapsed state with

only one surviving portal stone and a gallery constructed of very large stones. Other examples of two portal tombs contained in the same cairn include Kilclooney More about 5 miles south-west, and Ballyrenan, Co. Tyrone.

TARA

County Meath

The legendary fame of Tara promises more to prospective visitors than it delivers. While its pre-eminence amongst ancient Irish sites is not in doubt, material evidence to support its reputation as a great prehistoric sanctuary and centre of Celtic kingship is disappointingly thin on the ground. Of Tom Moore's far-sung 'Tara's Halls' nothing remains save a number of earthworks bearing evocative but wholly spurious names concocted by nineteenth-century romanticists. There is little of megalithic significance here, either; however, one relic has acquired a celebrity far greater than its size and appearance would suggest. This is the *Lia Fail*, 'Stone of Destiny', a 5-feet high granite monolith identified as the inauguration stone of the High Kings of Tara. It stood originally beside the Mound of the Hostages, a late Neolithic passage tomb nearby, and it is entirely conceivable that a prehistoric standing stone of evident sanctity should have been adopted as a potent symbol of royal authority. It is said that the stone roared in approval when a new king-elect was presented to the people. Its phallic shape can scarcely be coincidental and it has been dubbed 'the most frequently visited Irish scion of a pagan fertility cult' by archaeologist Peter Harbison.

WOODTOWN

COUNTY DUBLIN

Hidden from view until one comes suddenly face to face with it, this astonishing megalith looms out of its ferny lair like some prehistoric monster lying in wait for the unwary. Known also as the Mount Venus dolmen, it lurks among the trees on the edge of a golf course 4½ miles south of Dublin and ¼ mile east of Woodtown road junction, where a gap in the hedge affords the most direct access.

Gabriel Beranger's 1781 watercolour of this portal tomb shows it in less claustrophobic surroundings, but no less ruined, with its awesome 45-ton granite capstone slumped against the one

standing portal stone, itself broken in two. The other of the pair now lies concealed in the undergrowth. When intact they would have lifted the capstone to a height of 15 feet or more above ground. Some of the less massive stones which formed the chamber were pillaged long ago for building material.

BRENANSTOWN

County Dublin

Known as the Glen Druid Dolmen after the narrow secluded valley in which it stands, 8 miles south-east of Dublin, this remarkable granite megalith was visited and sketched by Walter Harris about 1740, and by Gabriel Beranger in 1775, whose watercolour is reproduced above. Like several portal tombs in the Dublin area it is a large example of the class, with a chamber measuring 10 feet in length and up to 7 feet in maximum width. The mighty capstone, a tilted squarish block 15 feet by 15 feet and weighing perhaps 40 tons, is borne on half a dozen uprights, the front pair forming a portal with a traverse slab set between them. On the upper surface of the capstone two prominent grooves or channels are visible, diverging as they run down towards the back, one having twin ducts leading to the corner of the stone. They have evidently been artificially produced and appear to be drainage channels; but whether for carrying rainwater or, as proponents of druidism would have it, something more sanguinary, is anyone's guess.

BALLYLUMFORD

COUNTY ANTRIM

Whereas some megalithic monuments are difficult to find, this neat 'Druid's Altar' could hardly be more conspicuous or accessible: it even has an address, 91 Ballylumford Road, Islandmagee, the result of an unlikely juxtaposition of a house of the living alongside a house of the dead. When *The Dublin Penny Journal* published the accompanying woodcut in 1833, the tomb stood out as a solitary landmark at the relatively remote northern end of this peninsula. The present villa was built here later in the century and this 4000-year-old megalith became thoroughly domesticated, and is now a unique garden

eye-catcher trimmed with flowers round the base.

The dolmen is about 6½ feet high overall and consists of a horizontal capstone 6 feet long and 18 inches thick, perched on a rectangular chamber of four stout uprights, all basalt. It may be a portal tomb, but could equally be the remains of a small passage tomb. An early account states that it was formerly surrounded by a circle of standing stones, probably the revetment of a cairn, any trace of which has disappeared. A gold collar reportedly found here long ago is unlikely to have had any connection with the dolmen.

BROWNE'S HILL

County Carlow

Signposted 2 miles east of the county town of Carlow, in Browne's Hill demesne at Kernanstown, this prodigious dolmen may not be one of the most graceful, but it can claim the distinction of having the heaviest capstone of all, not only in Ireland but probably in Europe too. Borlase's round-figure estimate of 100 tons need not be disputed, though it inevitably allows for a margin of error either

way, since there is no way of calculating precisely how much it weighs. The massive granite block, measuring almost 20 feet along each side and 5 feet thick, rests on three 6-feet high orthostats at the front, forming a conventional portal and doorstone arrangement, while the back end is lifted clear of the ground on two low boulders. A free-standing upright to one side of the portal may be the remains of a forecourt façade. No other structural stones survive that would indicate the extent of the chamber or to show if there ever was a cairn.

Previous page: Front view of dolmen showing doorstone flanked by portals supporting the 100 ton capstone, with the façade stone on left.

EIGHTERCUA

COUNTY KERRY

Tradition has it that this is the burial place of Scéine, wife of Amergin, leader and warrior-poet of the legendary Milesian invaders who reached Ireland around 1700 BC. This, fortuitously, would agree with the general period of the megalith. A prominent landmark on a ridge high above the road 1 mile south-south-east of Waterville, overlooking Ballinskelligs Bay, this four-stone alignment extends 25 feet in a roughly east to west direction. The tallest stone is a little over 9 feet in height. There are indications that this may have been more than a simple alignment: traces of an ancient enclosure

adjoining it, now much depleted, and remains of a possible megalithic tomb suggest a ritual purpose for this site. Observations have shown that the stones are orientated towards the setting sun at the winter solstice.

CLONTYGORA

County Armagh

Even though it has suffered at the hands of despoilers in the past and been robbed of many of its stones, this great court tomb, 'The King's Ring', remains one of the most imposing monuments of its type in Northern Ireland. Set amid some fine south Armagh scenery close to the border with the Republic, 4 miles south of Newry, it is reached by a minor road leading off the main Newry-Dundalk road at Killeen (if asking directions the local pronunciation is 'Clinchycora'). Sited on a little plateau on the south side of a valley and somewhat unusually facing north, the U-shaped forecourt leads to a burial gallery extending south behind large well matched portal stones. Substantial as these are they are dwarfed by a magnificent pair of flanking orthostats standing over 8 feet tall. Indeed, everything about this tomb has a monumental quality that cannot fail to impress and a visit is highly recommended.

Only the first chamber survives relatively intact, with its

huge capstone still raised aloft over a displaced lintel. The chamber sides are formed by massive split-granite boulders, and further large horizontally laid stones mark what remains of the second and third chambers. Of the original cairn little is to be seen, most of its stones having been removed in the 1730s for the construction of the first lock on the Newry canal. The megalith was again plundered a century later when some of the larger stones were earmarked for a similar project. Fortunately for archaeology an accident resulted in the contractor relenting before irreparable damage was done. Two rusting iron wedges embedded in the north face of the westernmost flanker remain as evidence of this act of vandalism. An information board at the site has a conjectural reconstruction of the monument, as well as illustrations of artifacts recovered during excavation in 1937.

BURREN

County Cavan

There are several places called Burren in Ireland in addition to the famous limestone karst region of Co. Clare, and since the word simply means 'a rocky place' its frequency is hardly surprising. This particular Burren is a mountainous townland to the south of Blacklion village and contains a number of notable megalithic remains, including this remarkable structure standing in a forest clearing. At first all one notices is a huge slipped capstone, 16 feet long, steeply pitched with one end resting on the ground, its scabrous surface colonised by mosses and lichen. Close inspection reveals that this unusual monument has been greatly altered, almost beyond recognition from its original form. When Borlase saw it in the 1890s it had been converted to use as a 'calves' house' by building up the open sides with masonry. Many megalithic tombs were utilised as animal shelters in times past, but few have been so extensively modified. It is not possible therefore to reconstruct the chamber plan; however, a pair of 7-feet tall orthostats, against the northern of which the displaced capstone leans, identify it as a portal tomb of classic type, and, as Borlase rightly observed, 'it must have been an unusually fine one'.

On an elevated site among trees about ¼ mile east of the dolmen and reached by a rough grassy track, is a large well-preserved wedge tomb. Five horizontal capstones remain in place over a long,

Above: Dolmen in the forest; only the tomb entrance is visible in the overgrown cairn

Right: Another view of the dolmen on previous page. Modern masonry used to convert it to an animal shelter can be seen between the portal stones, against which the dislodged capstone leans

low gallery divided into antechamber, main chamber and a small end chamber. Two sturdy orthostats at the south-west lean towards each other to form an entrance shaped like an inverted V. Some double-walling survives along the sides of the gallery. Nearly ½ mile south-west of here, hidden in the forest, is a perfect small portal tomb still buried in a cairn overgrown with heather and bracken. Only the front edge of the capstone is visible, resting on the open portal through which one can peer into the gloom of the chamber.

CHURCHTOWN

County Tyrone

A modern field-wall intrudes on this despoiled but not unimpressive megalith, still clearly recognisable as a single-chamber portal tomb. It lies ½ mile north-north-east of Castlederg, nearly 150 yards to the east of Lurganboy road. Like many such monuments it is known as the 'Druid's Altar'. A large displaced capstone is slumped against the east side of the chamber, apparently having been 'wantonly overturned by some barbarian' sometime prior to 1872. One of the portal stones which supported it is missing, evidently removed for building stone. A secondary capstone rests *in situ* at the back of the chamber, so this was probably a dolmen of the double-capstone variety similar to the Kempe Stones in Co. Down.

About ¼ mile north-east of this megalith is 'Todd's Den', a Bronze Age wedge tomb with a gallery measuring 22 feet in length by 4 feet wide, whose roofstones are fallen and some of the sidestones displaced.

GLACKADRUMMAN

Above: Sheep graze among the remains of Ireland's most northerly stone circle

COUNTY DONEGAL

Few stone circles are recorded from Ireland's most north-westerly county, and perhaps only two can be identified with certainty; several possible sites lie partly buried in peat bog and have not been fully investigated. Glackadrumman circle occupies a prominent position on windswept Mass hill (so called from its use as a place of clandestine worship in Penal times), 1 mile from Culdaff village, and is sometimes known by its old name Bocan, or Banchan, from *bainseachan*, meaning pastureland, which it still is. A ring of perhaps thirty stones originally, with a diameter of 65-70 feet, its despoiled state is the result of land clearance for agriculture in the early nineteenth century. Many stones were removed and others buried where they were overthrown. Fortunately the scheme was never completed, but a number of potentially important finds within the enclosed area were not preserved. Seven stones up to 6 feet in height remain standing and a few are prostrate. Before its mutilation this must have been one of the more impressive megalithic rings in the country and as significant archaeologically as those of the south-west Munster series.

This location is one of scenic beauty and affords good views of Inishowen. On a neighbouring hill is Laraghirril Cairn, otherwise popularly called 'The Temple of Deen', a ruined court tomb of which about twenty stones survive.

CLONFINLOUGH

County Offaly

This large solitary boulder, known as 'The Fairy's Stone' and 'The Horseman's Stone', lies in a field adjacent to Clonfinlough church, less than 3 miles east of Clonmacnoise. It is decorated with a profusion of unusual designs, some of which are thought to represent human figures, as well as other devices including cup-marks which may date the scribings, if the various elements are contemporary, to the Bronze Age. Expert examination of the surface has shown that the 'figures' were produced by embellishing natural solution pits with a simple incised line that is very beautiful in its effect. The compostion as a whole suggests a scene of vigorous activity, and it has been interpreted by some as depicting a great prehistoric battle. On the other hand, it may be nothing more than the work of a casual doodler whiling away the time. In either case, this is an intriguing piece of ancient stylised art that could equally pass as modern art. Comparable anthropomorphic

Above: A tall portal stone, left, flanks a doorstone, with the stump of the broken east portal stone beside it.

Right: Plan and section

designs are found in parts of Spain, but this is the only known Irish example, apart from a stone bearing somewhat similar decoration in one of the satellite tombs at Knowth in Co. Meath.

AGHMAKANE

COUNTY ARMAGH

'The Long Stones' occupy an elevated site in Aghmakane townland (pronounced 'Ahmakane'), 1½ miles south-west of Camlough and several hundred yards south of the road to Milltown. Access is difficult due to the heavily overgrown and at times marshy nature of the surrounding fields. The megalith, formerly known as 'The Hag's Chair', stands close to a small cashel of much later date, now almost obscured by gorse. Despite much mutilation The Long Stones are recognisable as a remnant of a large portal tomb, though the hilltop siting is somewhat unusual. In its present state it consists of two tall pillars of granite alongside the broken stump of a third stone. The west stone of the group is 9½ feet high and leans slightly: the middle one, which is aligned at right angles to its fellows, is 7 feet high. This arrangement of the stones, as shown by the plan, is in keeping with the idea of a doorstone flanked by a pair of tall portal stones, assuming that the broken east stone originally matched the height of the west one.

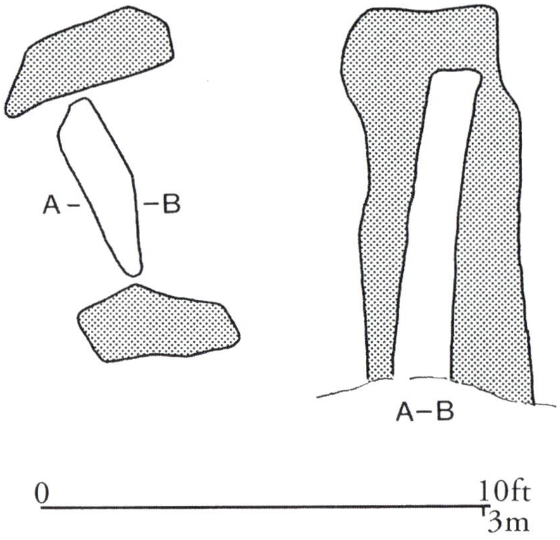

It is likely that the chamber and cairn served as a stone quarry for the construction of the cashel, and a massive recumbent slab inside its walls is almost certainly the missing capstone. One might speculate as to how the portal stones survived the depredations of the cashel builders; it may simply be that they were too difficult to manhandle, or just not required – or were they perhaps left untouched as a token mark of respect for an already ancient and to some extent still revered monument?

This must once have been a very impressive structure indeed, comparable in size with some of the tallest dolmens in the country. Its closed portal features are strongly reminiscent of those at Knockeen (Waterford) and Kilmogue (Kilkenny).

THE LIOS

COUNTY LIMERICK

Many of Ireland's early monuments have the power to evoke a sense of mystery, few more so than this great stone circle, the largest in the country, 12 miles south-south-east of Limerick and 900 yards to the west of Lough Gur, in an area noted for its wealth of prehistoric remains. The Lios is a 100-feet diameter megalithic ring of standing stones set contiguously inside a wide earthen bank, 3 feet high and heavily tree-grown, through which a paved passageway on the east leads to an entrance flanked by prominent portal stones.

Among the orthostats lining the interior of the bank is one

which stands head and shoulders above the rest: the monumental squared pillar known as 'Crom Dubh', the pagan god who presided at the festival of Lughnasa. It is 8 feet tall with a further 5 feet buried below ground and is believed to have been brought here from a source over 1 mile away, a formidable task that would have called for a large and highly organised workforce. The builders of this splendid arena were clearly concerned with appearance and attention to detail: as a cosmetic finishing touch they carefully levelled the interior with a deep layer of clay and gravel which also served to conceal the packing stones around the base of the orthostats. Excavation yielded much pottery, and stone tools and other artifacts, and provided dating evidence of use around 2000-1800 BC. This was essentially a place of ceremony in the early Bronze Age and, judging from its size and complexity, one of considerable importance.

BALLYNAGEERAGH

COUNTY WATERFORD

There are a number of well-preserved portal tombs of the distinctive double capstone type in south-east Ireland, and this one, 5 miles west-south-west of Tramore, is a particularly handsome example despite recent unsympathetic restoration which has encumbered it with an ugly concrete surround. The poise of the large capstone is well conveyed in this pair of nineteenth-century sketches, observed from different angles. The 12 by 8 feet slab balances on just two supports, a tall upright stone closing the entrance on the north-west, and a smaller secondary capstone resting across the sidestones

THE BROAD STONE

COUNTY ANTRIM

of the compact rectangular chamber. This is a good area for megalith exploring: the fine dolmens of Knockeen and Gaulstown, as well as Matthewstown wedge tomb all lie within a few miles of each other.

Above: The Broad Stone. The reinstated capstone is supported by the portal stones and backstone of the first chamber

This striking example of a Neolithic court tomb is situated in Craigs townland and lies at a height of 614 feet on the west side of Long Mountain, a conspicuous hump of moorland pasture rising abruptly from the Bann lowlands north of Rasharkin. It nestles in a hollow beside a thorn tree and is fenced in to protect it from grazing livestock. The remains are in a fair state of preservation and comprise a three-chambered gallery segmented by jambs, an almost semi-circular forecourt 18 feet in diameter, facing south-east, and a number of kerbstones delimiting the long cairn. Its most notable feature, the great 10 by 8½ feet capstone, had

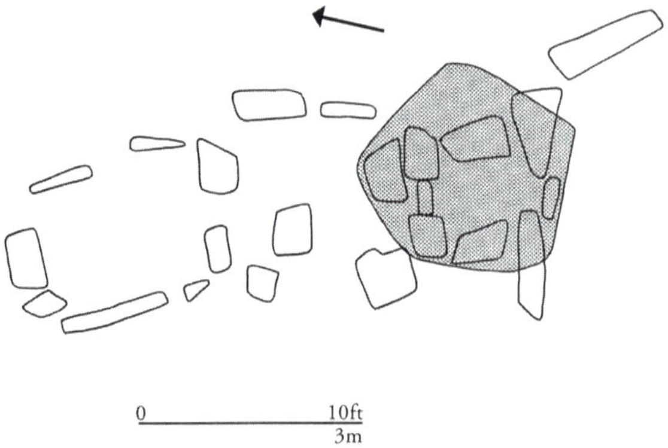

Above: Plan of Gallery with replaced capstone over first chamber

collapsed or been overthrown sometime prior to 1816 (when Mason's *Statistical Survey of Ireland* records it fallen), but was replaced late in the nineteenth century by the concerted efforts of the local population, a task said to have taken a week to complete. At that time the megalith was a well-known focal point for community gatherings and merrymaking.

While the position of the reinstated capstone over the first chamber is probably authentic, the tall supporting upright at the back which gives it the appearance of a classic 'tripod dolmen' must be regarded as suspect, since it contravenes the normal rules of court tomb construction. On the other hand it could conceivably be an aberrant original feature, given the recognised transitional link between court and portal tombs.

CRAIGS

County Antrim

About ½ mile south-west of the previous entry, over a stile into a field on the west side of Mullan road, is the well-preserved chamber of a small, neatly constructed passage tomb whose 8 feet by 5½ feet capstone was shattered in the 1970s as a result of rainwater freezing in faults in the basalt. It was repaired during excavation in 1985 and replaced in its original position on the seven uprights forming the oval chamber. The underside of the capstone was found to have a number of grooves, artificially cut, to allow it to rest securely on the supporting stones – a feature noted also at Magheraboy passage tomb on the north Antrim coast. Until the nineteenth century this megalith retained most if not all of its cairn, with the capstone alone being the only visible part of the structure. There may have been a short passage in front of the entrance, which faces west-south-west, but this feature is often lacking in northern versions of the type.

ISLAND

County Cork

Fairly well-preserved remains of a wedge tomb situated on farmland 5½ miles south-south-east of Mallow. Many of the structural stones survive, but the covering cairn depicted in the conjectural reconstruction below had all but disappeared long before the tomb was excavated half a century ago. Features still present include several tall orthostats of the straight façade, and a long, partially roofed gallery forming a single chamber. The usual double-walling of this type of tomb is well displayed. The only finds – some fragments of cremated bone – came from a pit in the floor of the gallery. The cairn shape was round, as revealed by the discovery of empty sockets which once held a ring of small standing stones outlining its limits. Further sockets forming a curved line in front of the gallery indicated that earth or stones had been piled up here to block the entrance and conceal the megalithic façade from view.

OWENEA

County Donegal

Even though it is over 9 feet tall, this impressive pillarstone often goes unnoticed as it is partly hidden behind a derelict cottage to the south of the river at Owenea bridge, which is 1 mile north of Ardara. It is remarkable for its uniformity and measures approximately 4 by 2½ feet in plan. While a few comparable examples occur around the Mourne Mountains, monoliths on this scale are fairly rare in northern counties. The finest are found in Kildare and in parts of south-west Munster, some standing to heights in excess of 15 feet. Some solitary pillarstones have been shown to be remnants of more complex monuments, and it is possible that this one could be the sole surviving portal stone of a destroyed dolmen, or part of an alignment.

CREEVYKEEL

Above: Creevykeel. View of the chambered gallery from rear, looking towards the court

County Sligo

This splendid megalith is one of the finest examples of a dual-court tomb and, thanks to meticulous restoration following excavation in 1935, it provides visitors with a very clear understanding of the layout and construction of these complex monuments. It has the added advantage of being readily accessible, lying only yards to the east of the main Bundoran to Sligo road at the crossroads hamlet of Creevykeel. The oval court is 50 feet in length and is entered by an orthostat-lined passage on the east. Directly opposite, at the west end of the court, a shallow curved façade leads to the lintelled entrance of a long gallery, now roofless, divided by massive jambs into two chambers. Beyond these in the west end of the wedge-shaped cairn, is a pair of subsidiary chambers set back to back and aligned north/south, entered via short passages leading in from the sides of the cairn. They resemble small passage tombs in plan and may have been added somewhat later, as was possibly a further chamber whose scant remains lie near the end of the cairn. Cremated burials and grave goods recovered during

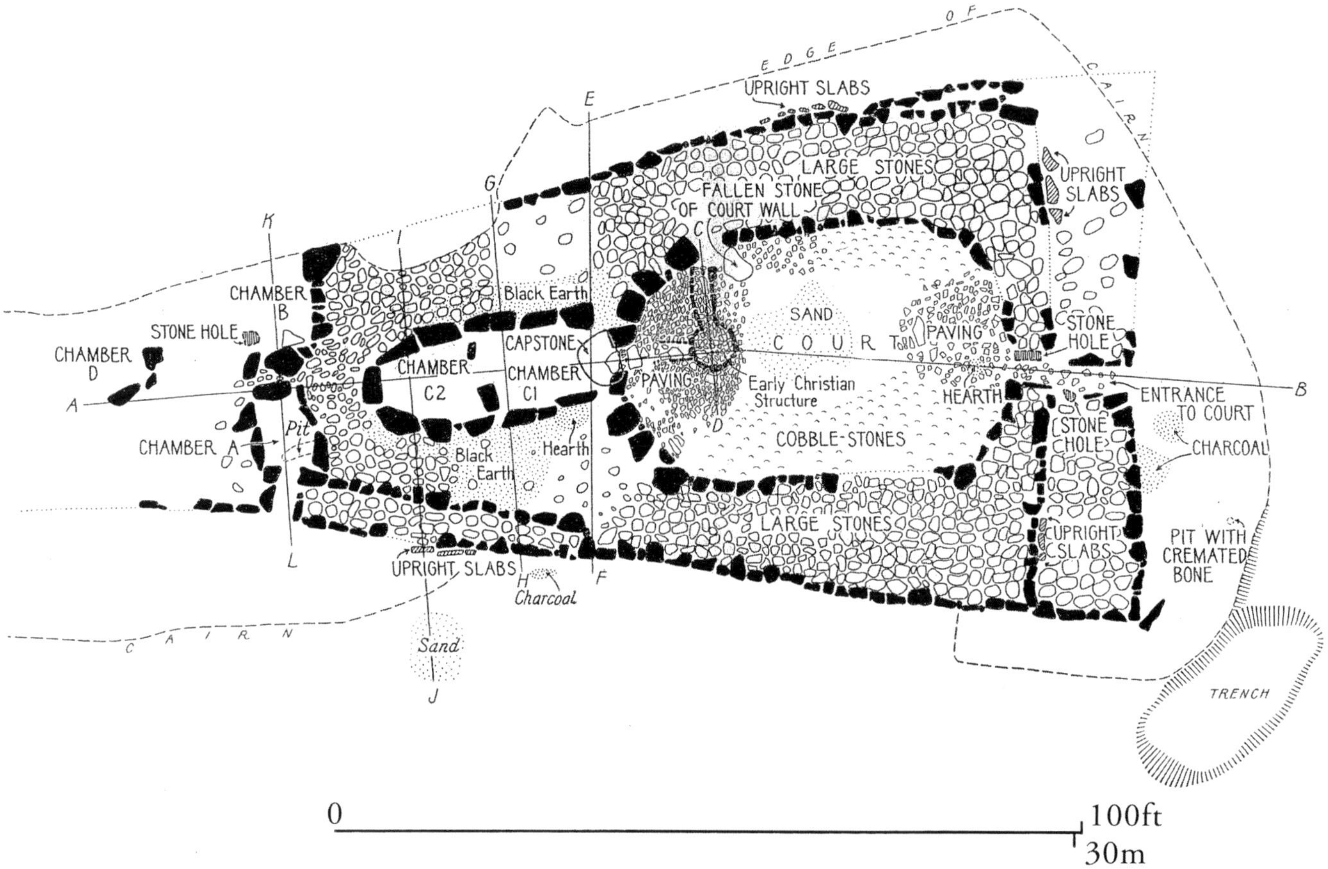

excavation indicated a late Neolithic date of around 2500 BC. In early Christian times the court was appropriated for utilitarian use and an iron-smelting kiln constructed in one corner. Objects associated with domestic activity were recovered from this area.

Above: Plan of Creevykeel court tomb. The gallery, court and kerb stones are shown in black. The court entrance is on right of plan.

PARKNABINNIA

COUNTY CLARE

The rocky landscape of The Burren has an astonishing concentration of wedge tombs within its boundaries – nearly a hundred have been recorded, accounting for a sixth of the total number in the entire country. Many are difficult to find as they tend to blend into their grey surroundings, and it is worthwhile obtaining the excellent large-scale map of the region produced with painstaking attention to detail by Tim Robinson and sold locally. It is an indispensable aid to serious exploring, marking not only megalithic sites but also the rich variety of other early remains to be found here.

Parknabinnia is one of the more accessible wedge tombs, visible to the west of the road 1¼ miles north of Killinaboy. It is a well-preserved and very typical example which displays the neat box-like construction achieved by the use of long slender slabs of limestone to form the side walls and roofstone. Unlike wedge tombs in other areas, there is no antechamber to the gallery, which is unsegmented and closed at each end. The grass-grown layer of earth and stones on top is the remains of the cairn which once completely covered the structure.

CASTLERUDDERY

County Wicklow

A large, almost 100-feet diameter despoiled stone circle, nearly 5 miles north-east of Baltinglass at the approach to the Glen of Imail. Unusually, it is contained within a low earthen bank, 15 feet wide and faced with stones, on and around which rowan and elder trees grow, adding to the slightly mysterious atmosphere of the place. Most of the circle stones are fallen and lie in disarray in the undergrowth, but a few shapely orthostats stand out. Also clearly identifiable are the massive recumbent portal stones, two gleaming quartz blocks each 9 feet in length. There is also what appears to be the remains of a short entrance passage leading into the circle from the east. Aerial survey of the site revealed traces of a large outer work of fosses and banks which mark this as an especially complex monument, undoubtedly ritual in purpose and possibly a hybrid version of a henge. Even in its present state of decay it is deserving of conservation.

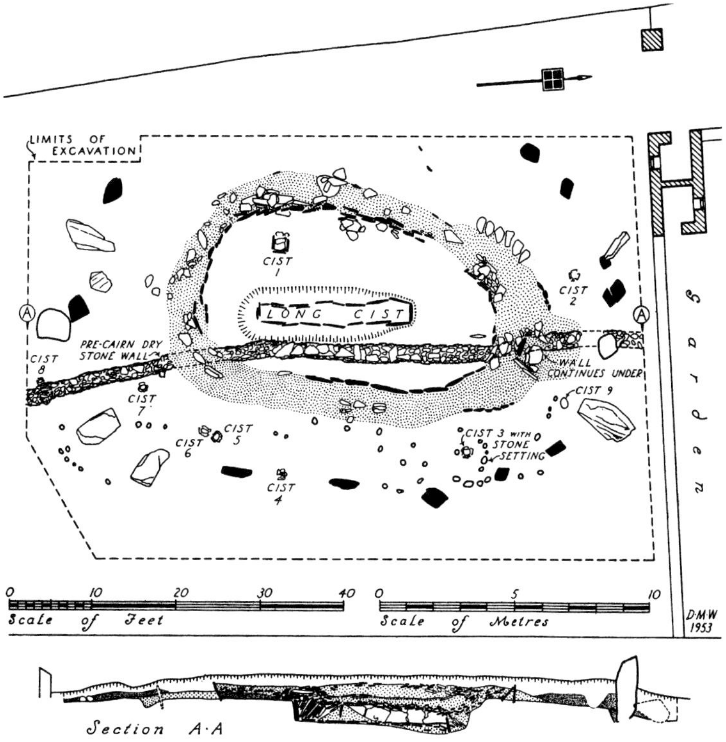

MILLIN BAY

Above: Millin Bay. Plan and section

COUNTY DOWN

There is little to see at this important archaeological site, since after excavation in 1953 the sandy mound which covered it was replaced to protect its unusual features, leaving only the outer ring of tall standing stones on view. It is situated close to the shore at Millin Bay, 2½ miles south-east of Portaferry. The mound is oval in plan and is cut through on its long north-south axis by a low dry-stone wall which was shown to be older than the structures built around it. For whatever reason, it was evidently held in sufficient reverence to be incorporated in the burial monument. To the west of it was a well-constructed long cist containing the bones of numerous individuals. It was mounded over with shingle and isolated from other features by a revetment of thin slabs, very many of which were decorated in the style of passage tomb art, but with a limited range of motifs. A number of small cists were located near the edge of the main mound, and in this area also were deposited smooth ritual stones called baetyls. A late Neolithic date seems probable for this hybrid monument, but some features hint at Bronze Age influences.

NEWGRANGE

COUNTY MEATH

Splendidly situated on a grassy height overlooking a wide sweep of the River Boyne, 7 miles south-west of Drogheda, Newgrange passage tomb is one of Ireland's best known and most written about visitor attractions. Entrance to the site is by the tourist office and interpretative centre nearby, at Donore. It is open to the public Monday to Saturday and the modest admission charge includes a guided group tour of the chamber.

Built around 3200 BC, Newgrange represents monumental architecture on a scale not witnessed elsewhere in western Europe at that time. The great mound, nearly 300 feet in diameter and over 35 feet in height, is retained by a kerb of massive horizontal stones, many bearing decorative devices. The magnificent entrance stone was probably carved *in situ* and displays the unique triple spiral motif found only at Newgrange. A box-like construction above the entrance was initially thought to be a facility for passing offerings through to the dead, but its astonishing secret was later revealed when observations found that its purpose was to allow the sun's rays to penetrate the passage and illuminate the burial chamber on 21 December, the winter solstice.

A 62-feet long passage lined with huge orthostats and roofed with lintels, leads to the cruciform chamber, whose roof of skilfully laid courses of corbelling rises to a height of 19 feet at the centre. Each of the side chambers has decoration of a high quality, and the triple spiral appears again, this time on one of the jambs of the western recess. Two of the chamber recesses contain a single ritual stone basin on the floor, while the northern one has a double basin with two small hollows in the uppermost one, presumably to hold liquid offerings.

Long after the completion of the tomb, perhaps a thousand years later, Beaker people arrived here and erected a great circle of standing stones around the mound. Twelve out of a possible thirty-eight survive, the most imposing of which are on the east side in front of the entrance. It is to be noted that the façade of gleaming white quartz is modern, a conjectural construction intended to show how the mound might have looked originally. The stylised interpretation has attracted a fair amount of criticism from those who consider it to be restoration taken too far, but it cannot detract from the integrity of the interior, and the feeling it evokes of stepping back into prehistory.

Top Left: Triple spiral motif on sidestone of western chamber
Top Right: Detail of corbelled roof of main chamber

Bottom: Decorated stone in front of tomb entrance

CARROWKEEL

COUNTY SLIGO

A series of cairn-crowned ridges visible from afar marks the site of an important Neolithic tomb complex in the desolate Bricklieve Mountains to the west of Lough Arrow. There are fourteen cairns in total, some measuring up to 100 feet in diameter with cones 20 feet high. Two of the cairns lack burial chambers and two others contain simple megalithic cists, while another incorporates court tomb features in its construction. The majority however harbour passage tombs, and the two most typical examples (identified in archaeological literature as cairns G and K) have cruciform chambers of classic Irish form. Excavation a century ago yielded a variety of grave goods: pendants, bone pins, beads and decorated pottery of a type which became widely known as Carrowkeel Ware, from its first discovery at this site.

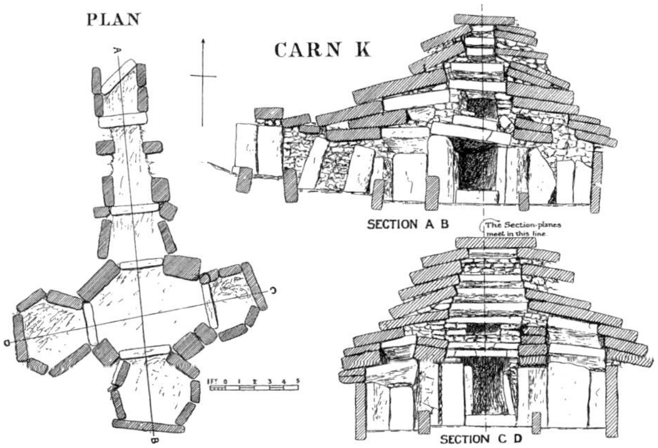

This is a bleak and lonely place, a monotone world of fissured limestone and dark bog against which the cairns stand out in stark isolation. The site is typical of the prominent hilltop locations favoured by passage tomb builders and, as might be expected, the views from it are extensive and breathtaking. It is perhaps significant that the great cairn on the summit of Knocknarea far to the north can be seen from here.

MONEYDORRAGHMORE

COUNTY DOWN

'The Long Stone' is a conspicuous and fondly regarded landmark in the townland of Moneydorraghmore, a remarkable world of massive boulder-built field walls 1¼ miles west of Annalong. Clearly visible from some way off, it presents a striking silhouette against the sky on a hill crest to the north side of Longstone road. Standing over 8 feet tall, the angular pillarstone is, despite the clutter of modern buildings around it, one of the most picturesquely sited of the numerous standing stones found about the Mourne Mountains, whose south-eastern flank of varied peaks provide an inspiring backdrop. Standing stones seem to have fared better than other early monuments in this district, notably court tombs which were often shamelessly exploited by granite workers as a ready source of building material. One would like to think that the survival of this Long Stone is due to local respect for a noble megalith.

ACHILL

COUNTY MAYO

Achill is the largest Irish island and one of the few to preserve much by way of a megalithic heritage. Its antiquities came under general notice in 1838 when the first Ordnance Survey of the area was carried out. Around the same time Caesar Otway mentions a number of these monuments in *A Tour in Connaught*, and later that century Col. Wood-Martin listed no fewer than eleven sites in the island as megalithic. The most authoritative work on the subject is the 1950 survey undertaken by Ruaidhri de Valéra and Sean Ó Nualláin, who identified four sites, while other previously supposed ones were either not megalithic in origin or could not be traced. It is likely however that some had been demolished for building stone in the interim. The surviving monuments, three court tombs and a portal dolmen, are all in ruin and not that easy to find, being overgrown and partly buried in bog; so a visit is recommended only to those with time to explore at leisure – and enjoy the natural beauty of the island as a bonus.

Above: Collapsed portal dolmen, townland of Dugort West

KILNASAGGART

COUNTY ARMAGH

This famous stone, standing 7 feet tall within a hedged enclosure in Edenappa townland, two fields in from the road and 1¼ miles south of Jonesborough, is virtually all that survives of an obscure early monastic site. The slender granite pillar has all the appearance of a prehistoric standing stone whose pagan origins have been disguised with the symbols of Christianity. Those responsible for its religious conversion did a thorough job, liberally decorating both sides with a total of thirteen inscribed crosses in a variety of designs. The stone is unique among early Christian monuments in that it can be reliably dated to about 700 AD from clues contained in a dedication in Old Irish script on the south-east face. A considerable number of burials, some in stone cists, were uncovered close to the pillar during excavation last century, suggesting that this was a cemetery adjoining the monastic settlement.

SRAHWEE

COUNTY MAYO

The name Tobernahaltora by which this wedge tomb is known, is a legacy of Penal times when it was visited as a holy well and altar. It stands immediately to the north of the road close to Lough Nahaltora, 6 miles south of Louisburgh. Many of the usual wedge tomb features are preserved despite some disturbance. The tapered shape of the gallery is well defined, with the large wafer-like capstone still in place. A doorstone, or septal slab, closes the entrance, which faces west, and some of the customary double-walling survives. The chamber is inclined to flood in very wet weather as water drains into it from a nearby ridge, and it was this phenomenon that led to the monument being adopted as a holy well.

BALLYRENAN

COUNTY TYRONE

Above: The western tomb; the capstone is supported on a slipped lintel which rests across the tops of the portal stones

This most interesting and accessible megalith stands beside a farmyard to the north side of Ballyrenan road, about 3 miles south-west of Newtownstewart. Occupying opposite ends of a long cairn orientated east/west are two portal tombs, the western one having a double chamber and two capstones, so angled as to resemble a pair of dolmens built back to back. Both capstones have worn cup-marks on their upper surfaces and are carried on lintels resting across the supporting uprights, an unusual form of megalithic construction for this class of monument. They cover two rectangular chambers which could be interpreted as separate units, or else a single segmented gallery. In the opinion of the excavator this western structure is secondary, erected perhaps not more than 100 years after the primary east tomb and possibly necessitating a partial reconstruction of the cairn to accommodate it. The cairn limits are traceable along much of its perimeter, except on the south-west where it is interrupted by the overgrown remains of a former road. The east tomb is very solidly built with massive side-stones to the chamber and imposing portal stones

Above: Interior of eastern tomb, looking east
Right: Portal stones at entrance to chamber

standing over 6 feet high. It is however roofless, having had its (apparently two) capstones displaced in the second half of the nineteenth century, presumably the work of treasure-seekers.

An exploration of the monument in 1907 organised by Lady Alexandra Hamilton of nearby Baronscourt House, produced 'seven large beads, four of them round and flat, and two long-shaped, of a greenish stone, and another very light and black – all perforated'. A more scientifically conducted excavation in 1936 recovered further artifacts including Neolithic pottery fragments, as well as cremated bone.

KNOCKEEN

County Waterford

This magnificent dolmen stands neglected and almost engulfed by a hedge in a corner of the disused burial ground of Kilburren, 4 miles south-south-west of Waterford city. It is a colossus, fittingly described by Borlase as 'remarkable for its solidity, and the perfect carrying out of a unity of design'. With a total height of 12 feet it is possibly the second tallest in Ireland, surpassed only by Kilmogue dolmen in Co. Kilkenny. The main capstone is a 12-feet long slab which overhangs the 9-feet high portal stones and rests at the back on a secondary horizontal capstone covering the rear of the rectangular chamber of six uprights. The tomb entrance faces west and is securely closed by a heavy doorstone almost as tall as the portal stones and recessed between them to form a portico.

GARRANE

County Cork

Linear settings of pillarstones are fairly numerous in the hilly country on the eastern margin of the Boggeragh Mountains, but are not easy to locate and access can be difficult. There is a palpable air of mystery about this hoary two-stone pair looming like ghosts out of the mist on a wooded spur of Bweengduff Mountain, some 2 miles north-west of Bweeng village. They are set about 6 feet apart and lean in opposite directions, and are aligned on a north-east/south-west axis, as are the majority of stone rows in the region. The northern stone is 8¾ feet high, the southern one 7½ feet.

Another fine and much more accessible pair can be seen at Monkey's Bridge, Glandine, about 1 mile to the south. The stones here are of similar height, the northern one again being the taller, with its southern counterpart set, unusually, at right angles. Stone pairs and multiple-stone alignments are broadly contemporary with the stone circle cult that flourished in the Bronze Age.

CARRICKGLASS

County Sligo

One would have to travel far to find a more eccentric legacy of the megalith builders than 'The Labby Rock': a Neolithic portal tomb of about 2000 BC, it stands at the bottom of a field near the north-eastern end of Lough Arrow, about 4 miles west-north-west of Ballyfarnan. Estyn Evans called it the clown among Irish dolmens, for there is surely something incongruous in the sight of its colossal 70-ton capstone bearing down on such seemingly inadequate supports, which look as though they might give way at any moment. Sporting an untidy mop of heather and grasses, this awesome limestone block is over 14 feet long and 7 feet thick, and is riven with faults and crevices. Beneath it, now unfortunately confused by a dry-stone wall built along one side, is a neat rectangular chamber measuring 6 feet by 3 feet and closed at the front by a slab set between the stubby portal stones. It has not been excavated in recent times, but cremated remains were recovered from the chamber more than a century ago.

DROMBEG

COUNTY CORK

This much publicised monument, 'The Druid's Ring', is one of the more accessible stone circles in the area, reached by a signed path 1½ miles east of Glandore. Its siting on a hillside plateau with views across small cultivated fields to the coast beyond is very beautiful. The circle has a diameter of 30 feet with an axis running north-east/south-west, providing an alignment on the mid-winter sunset. Its thirteen surviving stones – there were seventeen originally – are rather more closely set than in other West Cork circles. Several are truly megalithic, over 6 feet high, and some have smooth sloping tops, either artificially shaped or chosen for their appearance. The recumbent or axial stone is a long horizontal boulder with a flat upper surface bearing two cup-marks. At the centre of the circle excavators found an urn containing the cremated remains of a youth. Radio-carbon dating established that it was an early Iron Age burial of perhaps around 100 BC, which would be unusually late for

the erection of a stone circle, indicating a reuse of the monument at a much later date. Later still are the remains of domestic huts and an open-air cooking pit known as a *Fulacht Fiadh*, a short distance to the west of the circle.

Above: The recumbent, or axial stone is centre foreground, with the portal stones on the north-east quadrant directly opposite

Left: Drombeg stone circle from the north

Right: Ballynoe. Plan of stone circle and burial mound

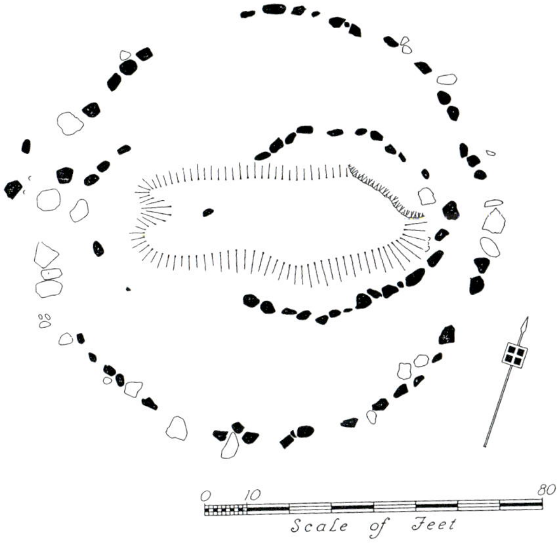

BALLYNOE

COUNTY DOWN

This hugely impressive monument, a combination of stone circle and long cairn or barrow, lies in the verdant Lecale peninsula less that 5 miles inland from Dundrum Bay. It is approached by a long, hedge-canopied lane leading west off Ballynoe road, 3 miles south of Downpatrick. An abundance of glacial erratics provided the circle builders with the materials for their monumental task. Fifty-five stones, mostly Octovician grit, form an almost perfectly circular megalithic ring 108 feet in diameter. Many are set contiguously, though some are fallen and a number are evidently missing. They

vary in size and shape with the tallest reaching over 6 feet on the north and south. Two of the fallen orthostats have deep cup-marks.

Standing outside the circumference of the circle on the west are two prominent stones which align with another pair to form a kind of double portal; the passageway through these leads to a raised semi-circular area of unknown significance immediately inside the circle. There are also several outlying monoliths at varying distances beyond the circle whose placing seems random, but which may be the result of intentional planning. The eastern part of the circle interior is occupied by a low elongated mound, partly kerbed, which harboured two large stone cists containing cremated bone. Altogether the remains of seven individuals were identified by the excavator. Also recovered were a number of water-smoothed sacred stones called baetyls, similar to those found at the Millin Bay site in Co. Down.

In some respects Ballynoe bears comparison with the stone circles of Cumbria, a relationship observed by Aubrey Burl in his survey of megalithic rings in different parts of the British Isles. The picture emerges here of a multiphase monument that began as an open ritual circle, possibly built early in the series, later taken over by newcomers to the area who adapted it to their own ritual customs. While it shares a number of features with Millin Bay, Ballynoe stands apart in its idiosyncrasy as one of the most imposing megalithic structures in Ulster, if not in all Ireland.

Above: Fallen orthostats on circle circumfrence, one with cup-marks

GAULSTOWN

COUNTY WATERFORD

A large and substantially intact example of a closed portal tomb of the distinctive Waterford group. It is situated on the wooded west side of Knockaghamaigh – meaning 'The Hill of the Foreigner' – slightly over 5 miles south-west of Waterford city. Six tall uprights form a hexagonal chamber measuring 7 feet by 5 feet internally, roofed with a 14-feet long capstone with a shaggy growth of grass and moss. It is uptilted to a height of 8½ feet above the entrance, which faces south-east. A tall doorstone is recessed between the portal stones to create a portico, a feature also seen to good effect at Knockeen dolmen 2 miles to the east. Nearby is a ruined wedge tomb.

PROLEEK

COUNTY LOUTH

This accessible and much visited megalith stands in the spacious grounds of Ballymascanlon House hotel, 3½ miles north-east of Dundalk and about 10 miles south of Newry. A classic 'tripod dolmen', it is known locally as 'the giant's load', since from the back it resembles a person stooped under a heavy burden, namely the great bulbous capstone estimated to weigh over 30 tons and delicately balanced on the pointed tops of 7-feet high portal stones and a slightly lower backstone. There is no formal chamber, and little evidence of a cairn. A whimsical custom still practised here requires a stone to be deftly tossed onto the top of the capstone without it rolling off the smooth convex surface; if accomplished, whoever threw it will wed before a year has elapsed.

An early illustration of this monument appeared in Thomas Wright's *Louthiana*, published in 1748. Wright recognised the sepulchral purpose of these structures and dismissed as fantasy the notion that they were druid's altars. He records that 'the native Irish tell a strange story about it, relating how the whole was brought all at once from the neighbouring mountains by a giant called Parrah Borg M'Shagjean, and who they say was buried near this place'. In contrast to Wright's instantly recognisable sketch, R. O'C Newenham's 1830 engraving in *Picturesque Views of the Antiquities of Ireland* presents a highly romanticised image of Proleek that is far removed from reality.

HOWTH

County Dublin

Known of old as 'Finn MacCoul's Quoits', this monstrous dolmen stands in the leafy environs of Howth castle, 1 mile south-west of the town. Beranger called it 'one of the grandest mausoleums', and while it certainly does impress one by its sheer size – the 70-ton, 17 by 12 feet capstone ranks second heaviest in the country – it has collapsed at the back, a state which prompted much debate in the nineteenth century as to whether it should be classed as an 'earthfast' dolmen, one whose capstone had always been in contact with the ground (the same case was also hotly argued for Woodtown, or Mount Venus, dolmen in the same county). The chamber is rather larger than in most portal tombs, extending to perhaps 12 feet in length, but its actual proportions are unclear.

Quite a number of megaliths are romantically linked with misty figures of prehistory. *The Cromlech at Howth* is the title of a long narrative poem by Sir Samuel Ferguson, who identified it as the tomb of the legendary heroine, Aideen:

They heaved the stone, they heaped the cairn
Said Ossian, "In a queenly grave
We leave her, 'mong her fields of fern,
Between the cliff and wave".

ANNAGHMARE

County Armagh

Surrounded by conifers of a state forestry plantation and approached by a lane to the east of a byroad, 2 miles north of Crossmaglen, this impressive monument has long been recognised as an outstanding example of an Irish court tomb. The imposing forecourt is seen today much as it must have appeared when it was built over 4000 years ago. A deep U-shape in plan with slightly incurving extremities, it well evokes the classic 'horned cairn' designation originally applied to this group of gallery tombs. Of particular interest and surviving here to a greater extent perhaps than in any other court tomb, are the very fine sections of dry-walling between the orthostats of the façade. This 'post-and-panel' construction consists of carefully bedded slabs of stone built up to bridge the gaps between the uprights, whose exposed faces are notably flat and evenly aligned. The well-preserved cairn, 65 feet in length, encloses a gallery of three chambers segmented by substantial angular jambs. The cairn survives in places to a height of over 5 feet and tapers markedly in width from south to north. It had been enlarged to accommodate two additional chambers set back to back at right angles to the

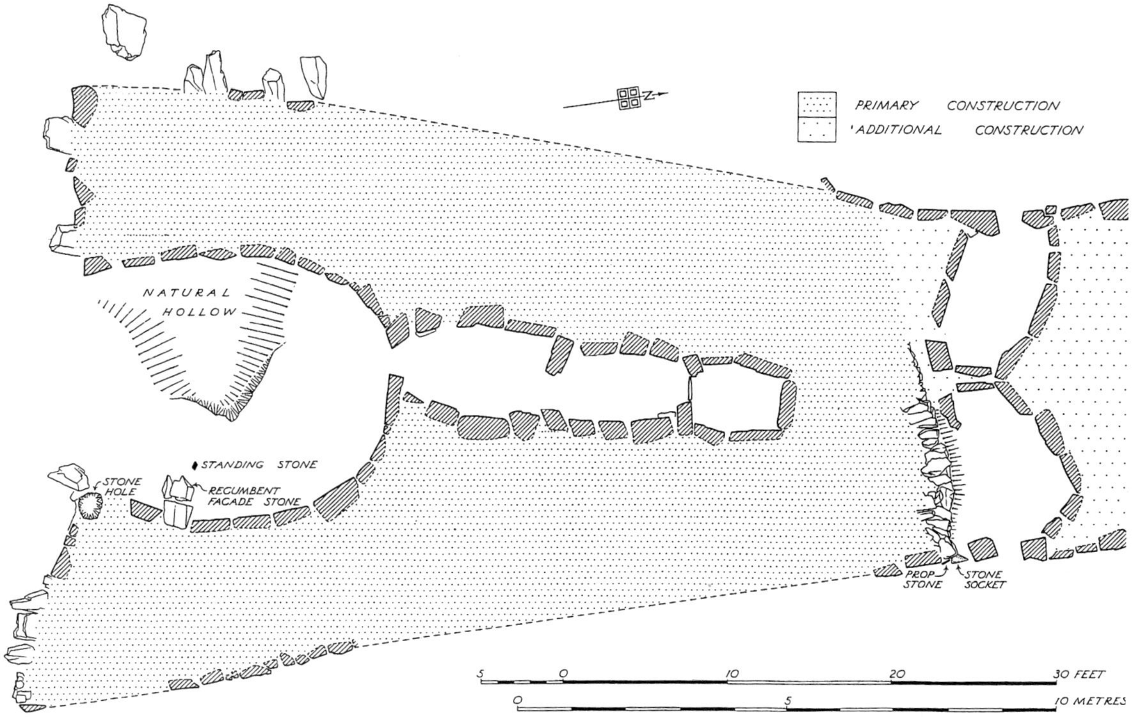

central gallery, the second and third chambers of which yielded cremated and inhumed remains, pottery and flints, when excavated in 1963-4. The megalith is known in the neighbourhood as the Black Castle and is marked such on older maps.

Previous page: Detail of court showing gallery entrance and dry-walling between orthostats

Above: Plan of Annaghmare court tomb and cairn. The horseshoe-shaped forecourt leads into a long gallery of three chambers, segmented by jambs. At some stage the cairn was extended at the back to accomodate two additional chambers

ARDMORE

COUNTY DONEGAL

A distinctive squared pillarstone of monumental proportions, standing about 7 feet high and heavily decorated on its south-east face with cup-marks, some surrounded by well executed single and multiple rings. No burials were found during excavation of the site in 1874, so this was probably an object of religious significance rather than a memorial to an individual. A novel explanation of the origin of the markings was volunteered to the excavator by local people: they were caused by stray cannon balls striking the stone during the siege of Londonderry in 1689!

Centuries of weathering in this exposed location has taken its toll and continuing deterioration seems inevitable, but this is still a singularly fine example of Galacian or Bronze Age art, well worth seeking out. The megalith is in a field adjoining a farmyard 1 mile north-north-east of Muff and is reached by a minor road leading west off the road to Moville. Permission to visit it may be obtained at the house.

SLIDDERYFORD

County Down

This conveniently situated 'tripod dolmen' can be seen from the main road from Dundrum to Newcastle, 1½ miles south-south-west of the former. It makes a striking object against the backdrop of the Mourne Mountains to the south-west. The field in which it stands is used for cultivation and the large ovoid capstone sometimes appears to be floating on a sea of waving wheat. Nearly 10 feet in length, it is supported on three of the four uprights which form the chamber. The north portal stone is considerably taller than the southern, but has a natural rebate or shoulder into which the convex underside of the capstone nestles, thereby compensating for the difference in height. There was formerly more to this site than now meets the eye. Writing around 1739, Walter Harris refers to 'a circle of Pillar-stones at Slidery-Ford in the C. of Down', and Dubourdieu mentions a ring of twelve standing stones here of which no trace remains. There is however a tall pillarstone several hundred yards to the south-west of the dolmen, possibly a remnant of a vanished court tomb.

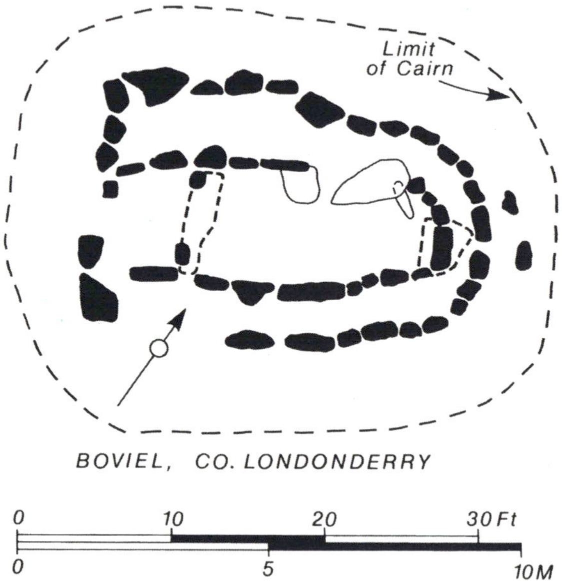

BOVIEL

COUNTY LONDONDERRY

A good example of a wedge tomb of the 'heel-shaped' northern type, lying at an altitude of 835 feet nearly 3 miles east-south-east of Dungiven. Its local name is Cloghnagalla, meaning 'Stone of the Hag', a reference to the Cailleach, or witch. The excavator of the site in 1938 was cautioned by local people that it was a place to be avoided at night, especially at Halloween when the apparition known as 'The White Lady' roamed here. Most of the ground plan of the monument is preserved. An antechamber at the south-west end of the cairn leads between side jambs to the now roofless burial chamber, 15 feet in length and composed of low basalt boulders. Outside this is a second row of stones set parallel to the line of the gallery, and the tomb entrance is flanked by a short straight façade whose tallest stones are placed at the extremities. Among an assortment of grave goods recovered was a fine polished axe.

TUROE

COUNTY GALWAY

Despite its uninspiring surroundings and the modern iron grating placed around it to fend off grazing sheep, this unique and beautifully decorated monolith is one of the great treasures of Celtic

La Tène art in Europe. The style of the carving, in its Irish context, is assignable to the last three centuries BC. Situated nearly 4 miles north-north-east of Loughrea, the Turoe Stone is a domed granite boulder standing a little over 3 feet high, artificially shaped and decorated by a technique known as pocking, which sets the design out in relief against the background. The abstract motifs comprise spirals, circles and curves, bounded by a band of simple step pattern carried round the lower part of the stone. The monument was removed to its present site from its place of discovery beside the Rath of Feerwore, an Iron Age ring-fort at Kiltullagh, a few miles away. Its phallic shape can hardly be coincidental and it may well represent a pagan fertility cult.

DRUMANONE

County Roscommon

Although not as aesthetically pleasing as some, this is nonetheless an impressive dolmen. It is situated in a field adjoining the railway line 2 miles west of Boyle, to the north-east of Lough Gara. A large example of the class, its portal stones stand between 7 and 8 feet high, with a tall doorstone set between them to close the entrance to the polygonal chamber. The massive capstone, over 14 feet in length east to west and 10 feet wide, is displaced and would originally have reached out beyond the portal. Excavation in 1954 recovered a porcellanite axe-head and evidence of cremations, but no other grave goods. Traces of a cairn of indeterminate outline survive.

CLOGHANMORE

County Donegal

Cloghanmore is the largest and one of the most interesting of the many megaliths scattered across this rugged coastal district, 2½ miles south-west of Glencolumbkille. The remains are of a fairly well-preserved full-court tomb sited in marshy ground close to a stream in Malin More glen. The oval-shaped court, about 45 feet long, combines orthostats and dry-walling, and leads to a pair of twin-chambered galleries built side by side at its western end, an arrangement found at only one other site: the magnificent full-court tomb at Magheraghanrush in Co. Sligo. Two small subsidiary chambers opening onto the east end of the court have faint traces of decoration on the entrance jambs, characteristic of passage tombs, but here unique in a court tomb context. The long tapered cairn, with its revetment of dry-walling was restored in a perfunctory tidying-up project in the nineteenth century and may not accurately represent its original shape.

About ½ mile west of Cloghanmore is a remarkable sequence of six dolmens set in line, apparently all at one time contained in the same cairn, which would have measured about

300 feet in overall length. Here and elsewhere in the district, some of the more commodious chambers have been appropriated by canny farmers for use as animal shelters. In 1871, a visitor to the imposing but mutilated megalithic tomb at Farranmacbride reported: 'On getting into another cavity, I found two black lambs inside, and in another some pigs, in another calves'.

GOWLANE NORTH

County Cork

This especially interesting but unfortunately mutilated stone circle lies in open pasture about 2 miles north of Donaghmore. The circle is of the West Munster type with an internal diameter of 21 feet, probably having nine stones originally. It is notable for the short entrance passage, demarcated by two radially aligned orthostats (one fallen) in front of the portals. The six stones still standing are about 3 feet in height, and the recumbent, or axial stone is a 4½ feet long rectangular slab set on edge opposite the portal stones, resulting in a north-north-east/south-south-west alignment through the centre of the circle.

This monument is under constant threat from cattle roaming between the stones and eroding the ground around their bases. As one of a small number of stone circles having the double portal feature noted above, its neglect is particularly deplorable and appropriate protective measures are urgently needed. Much of the damage is evidently recent, demonstrating how quickly deterioration can occur in a structure that has survived relatively intact for thousands of years.

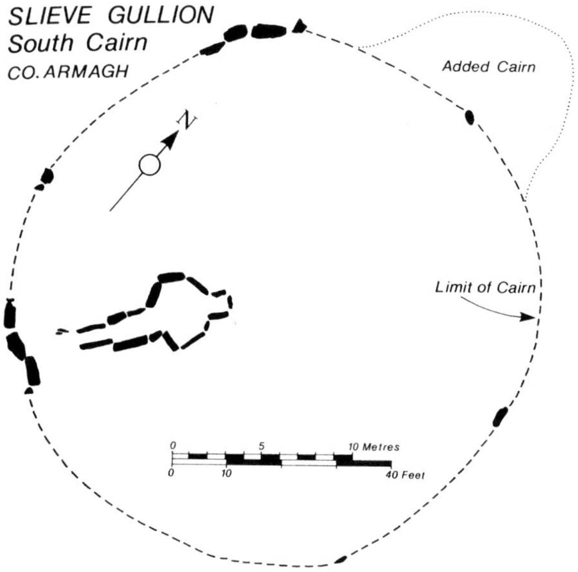

SLIEVE GULLION

COUNTY ARMAGH

The unmistakable hump of Slieve Gullion rises high in the middle of a volcanic ring dyke 5 miles south-west of Newry. On its exposed heathery summit, at 1894 feet, is the highest situated passage tomb in the British Isles, excavated in 1961 but known to have been ransacked long before. In folklore it is called 'Calliagh Birra's House', the abode of the Celtic Witch-goddess. A circular cairn with a diameter of about 100 feet is retained by a kerb of enormous stones which, contrary to the usual manner of passage tomb construction in Ireland, are laid with their broad faces flat to the ground rather than upstanding. A lintelled passage, reduced by collapse to 15 feet in length, leads to an octagonal chamber built of dry-walling which supports a corbelled roof, now largely destroyed. An alcove or auxiliary chamber opening off the north-east side of the main chamber may have had special significance since it is given prominence by a pair of flanking orthostats. Three roughly fashioned stone basins were found in the tomb, but neither they nor any of the chamber or kerb stones have decoration.

CALDRAGH

COUNTY FERMANAGH

Although it is not by definition megalithic, nor perhaps even prehistoric, this enigmatic stone idol seems to personify an ancient pre-Christian cult. It is as if the old gods still haunt the dank and melancholy environs of this disused burial ground on the south-

west shore of Boa Island in Lower Lough Erne. Two dwarf-like figures with disproportionately large heads and flat pointed faces gaze out from opposite sides of the 30-inch high stone, their baleful features delineated by boldly incised lines. The arms are crossed diagonally in front of the belted torsos, on one of which a phallus is indicated. On top of the stone, between the two heads, is a shaped cavity or socket which, it is conjectured, may have held an antlered headpiece, or served as a receptacle for ritual offerings. Whatever the origins of this curious piece of figure sculpture it is unlikely to be as old as the first century date sometimes claimed for it; but it does suggest a persistence of pagan customs well into the early Christian period in some of the more remote areas.

KILROOSKAGH

COUNTY FERMANAGH

One of the least known megaliths in the county, this collapsed dolmen is sited on a rocky outcrop at a height of 250 feet overlooking Lough Macnean Upper. It can be reached by a surfaced farm track leading uphill to the north of the road to Garrison, almost 2 miles north-west of Belcoo, then across fields to the right. Though it has sometimes been described as an 'earthfast' dolmen, on the suppostition that one end had always rested on the ground, there can be little doubt that it was once fully raised aloft on the chamber orthostats, several of which have given way under its weight.

The displaced capstone is a truly massive limestone slab measuring 15 feet in length and 9 feet in width, and up to 2 feet thick. The chamber stones are also extremely large, but are almost totally obscured by the brambly undergrowth. Even in its ruined state the monument can be recognised as a single-chamber portal tomb, and must have been a fine example of the class.

CONG

COUNTY MAYO

The district to the north-east of the village of Cong (well known for the fine carving in its Augustinian abbey, and even more so for its starring role in the film *The Quiet Man*) contains a wealth of prehistoric remains: cairns, stone circles, raths and cashels are to be found distributed over a wide area. James Ferguson and other nineteenth-century writers fancifully sought to identify these monuments with the so-called 'first battle of Moytirra', a mythological event enshrined in Gaelic legend. Sir William Wilde's *Lough Corrib, its Shores and Islands* (1867) illustrates two stone

circles, possibly those at Nymphsfield, traces of which may still be seen. Others are located in the adjoining townlands of Glebe and Tonaleeaun, some resembling the kerbs of cairns that have been removed, rather than ritual circles. Further to the north, Eochy's cairn is the largest prehistoric burial mound in the county and is presumed to harbour a passage tomb.

BALLYKEEL

COUNTY ARMAGH

The majestic profile of this 'tripod dolmen', to the east of Ballykeel road 4½ miles south-west of Camlough, recalls the classic lines of Legananny in Co. Down, and like it belongs to the late Neolithic period of tomb building, around 2500 BC. It is set in the south end of a cairn 94 feet in length and still 2 to 3 feet high, with its entrance facing south. To the east rises the cairn-crowned mass of Slieve Gullion, 'Ireland's most mysterious mountain', steeped in folklore and legends of the mighty Cúchulainn. The sturdy portal stones taper gracefully

to a height of nearly 7 feet and have a doorstone set between them blocking the entrance to half its height. There is no formal chamber however and the sides of the tomb may never have been fully enclosed. The great 9-feet long capstone had collapsed behind the portal when the rear support gave way sometime in the distant past, but was restored to its original position following excavation in 1963. A considerable amount of Neolithic pottery was recovered including 'Ballyalton bowls' (a type of decorated vessel with a distinctive shouldered rim, first recorded from a site in Co. Down). The north end of the cairn harboured a megalithic burial chamber or cist, the scant finds from which included a flint javelin.

Above: Ballykeel dolmen from east. Many of the kerb stones bounding the cairn remain in place

REANASCREENA SOUTH

COUNTY CORK

Heavily overgrown and hauntingly esoteric, especially at dusk when the last of the light slants across its lichened stones, this unusual stone circle lies 570 feet above sea level, 3 miles inland from Ross Carbery. Twelve evenly spaced uprights and an axial stone form a megalithic ring 30 feet in diameter, surrounded by a fosse and outer earth bank. The tallest stones are the matched portals on the east, directly facing the axial or recumbent stone at the opposite side of the circle. Excavation of the site in the 1960s revealed that the ground in the vicinity of the portals had been heavily eroded, and later reinforced with a layer of small stones, indicating much human activity in this area and probably, in the opinion of the excavator, the result of frequent processions or dancing. Several pits, one containing fragments of cremated bone, were found within and outside the circle. At some stage peat began to accumulate over the floor of the circle and in the fosse, possibly in the first millennium BC when climate change accelerated bog growth.

HAROLDSTOWN

COUNTY CARLOW

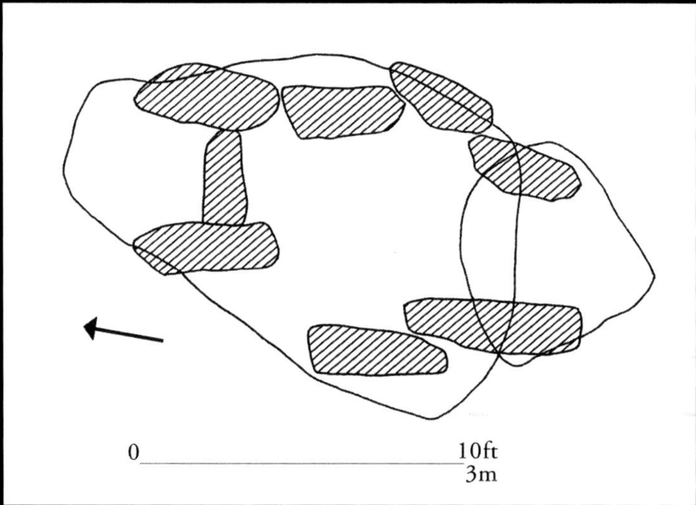

A well-preserved portal tomb beside the Derreen river 4 miles north-east of Tullow. It is in a field below Accuan bridge, which affords a good elevated view of the megalith, also known as the Tobinstown dolmen. The spacious chamber is relatively intact, lacking only one or possibly two sidestones, and measures 13 feet in length. It is covered by two large granite capstones, one of which is artificially grooved in the manner of several standing stones peculiar to the district. The chamber entrance is closed with a 6-feet high doorstone. The presence of an inquisitive horse in the photograph

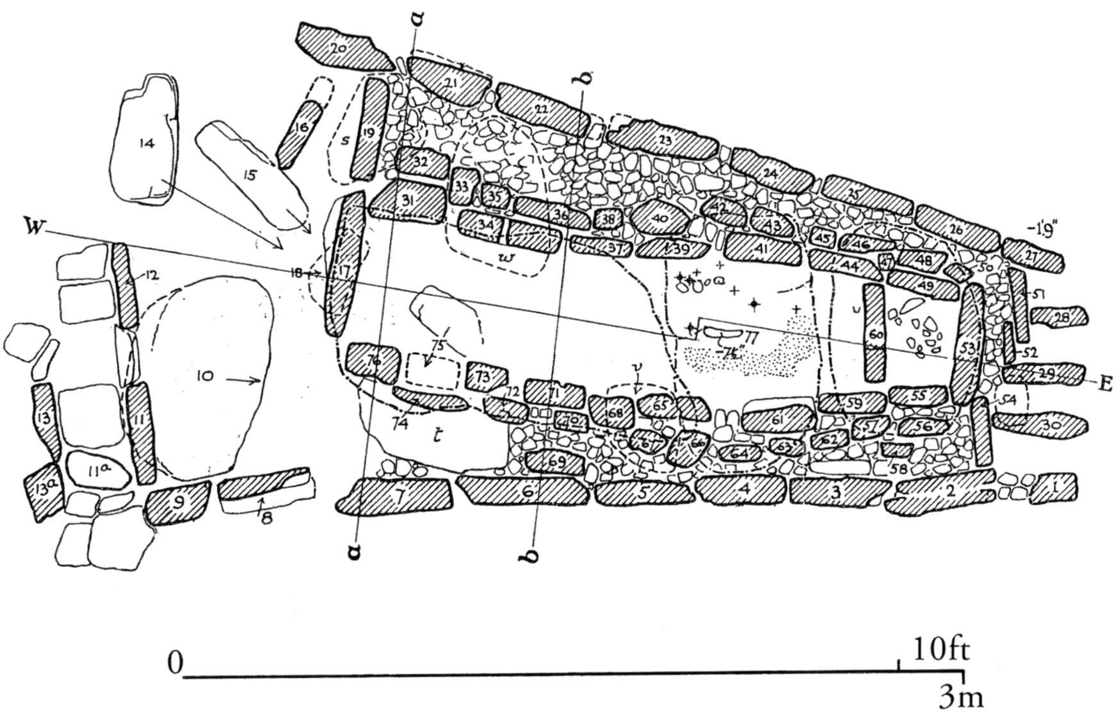

s a reminder that many such monuments were utilised as animal shelters in the past. More remarkable is the fact that this tomb was home to human occupants in the nineteenth century. Borlase states that 'a family at one time lived in this dolmen, which has a singularly house-like appearance, and in order to keep the cold out, plastered up the interstices with cob'.

Previous page: Plan of the Haroldstown dolmen

LABBACALLEE

COUNTY CORK

This well-known and relatively intact monument, beside a grove o trees 1¼ miles south-west of Glanworth, was excavated in 1934. I is the largest of all the Irish wedge tombs and exhibits very clearly the tapered shape, both in plan and long section, that gives the type its name. A noteworthy feature is the triple-walling of the gallery distinguishing it from the less elaborate double-walling found in the majority of wedge tombs – a mark of prestige, perhaps? The gallery is roofed with three capstones, the front one a colossal slab

on the west, which is blocked off from the unusually wide portico by a traverse slab between the jambs. In the main chamber the skeletons of an adult male and a child were found, along with a skull which was shown to belong to a headless female skeleton found in a small subsidiary chamber at the back of the gallery. The cairn has long disappeared but the stone kerb which bounded it survives in places.

THE GIANT'S RING

COUNTY DOWN

'Few things were more calculated to awe the mind and affect the imagination than this scene, when we contemplate it as a vast heathen temple, within the circuit of which many thousands of people may have assembled to witness the awful rites of their sanguinary religion.'

– J. B. Doyle
Tours in Ulster, 1854

Occupying a commanding position on a plateau to the east of the River Lagan in the townland of Ballynahatty, 4 miles south of Belfast, The Giant's Ring is the largest ceremonial enclosure in Ireland, a great prehistoric sanctuary and centre of ritual whose complexity and archaeological importance has only been fully recognised in the last couple of decades. It has for long been such a familiar landmark, much frequented by dog-walkers, joggers, courting couples and even cyclists, that it is easy to overlook just how impressive a monument this is.

A wide earthen bank up to 12 feet high encloses a roughly circular arena 7 acres in extent and 590 feet in diameter, intersected by five gaps, some of which are possibly original features. Much of the material for the bank was obtained by removing earth and stones from the inside perimeter, creating a slightly convex ground surface towards the centre of the enclosure. Where the bank meets the edge of the plateau on the east its arc becomes straightened out so that the ring is not perfectly circular; whether this was intentional or the result of an error in planning is open to conjecture. A megalithic chamber of five uprights supporting a large tilted capstone stands east of centre in the ring. No trace of a cairn survives but old reports of a circle of standing stones suggests a kerb, so this is possibly a passage tomb derivative and probably predates the earthwork.

Recent aerial survey of the site revealed traces of further structures to the north of the ring, and subsequent excavation uncovered the post holes of a large oval enclosure of massive timbers, with a second, circular enclosure of similar construction

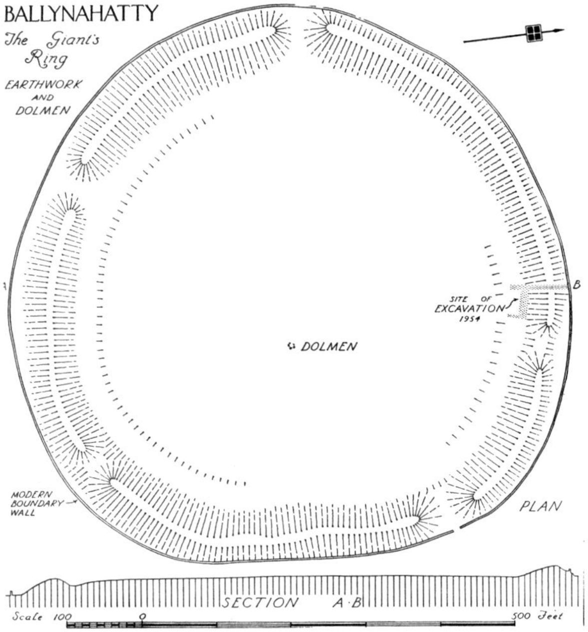

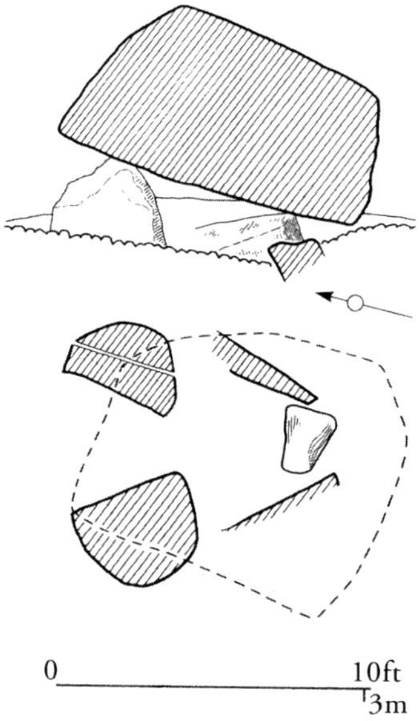

Above Left: Plan and section of the Giant's Ring

Above Right: Plan and section of Kilfeaghan dolmen

within it. This was interpreted by archaeologist Barrie Hartwell of Queen's University as a repository where bodies of the dead were left to decay or be defleshed in preparation for ritual burial. Perhaps J. B. Doyle was not so far off the mark after all. Certainly the scale and complexity of the site points to it having been a centre of immense social, political and religious significance, whose shadowy secrets are only now being slowly relinquished. It is a wonderfully atmospheric place. From the top of the bank one catches glimpses of an industrial city and its sprawling suburbs, but inside the ring all is quiet and still, and an old sanctity prevails.

KILFEAGHAN

COUNTY DOWN

The huge hump-back capstone of this ungainly dolmen, 4 miles east of Rostrevor, was probably an *in situ* erratic which was shored up to allow a chamber to be constructed underneath, since it is clearly too massive to have been transported any distance. Furthermore, the chamber cavity was hollowed out from the slope of the field rather than raised above ground level in the more usual manner. As long ago as 1883 William Gray wrote that 'the site has become a rubbish dump for ages, and all the loose field stones and other impediments to farming operations have been collected around the cromlech so far as to hinder the goats from taking shelter in the chamber as they were wont to do'. The accretion of stones around the chamber remains, greatly reducing the apparent height of the portal stones, which are in fact nearly 8 feet tall. It is recorded that the cairn previously extended about 25 feet north of the entrance, indicating that there may have been a forecourt, supporting the opinion of some archaeologists that portal tombs and court tombs are related.

ANNACLOGHMULLIN

COUNTY ARMAGH

'The gradual decay, and, in too many instances, the complete destruction of our ancient monuments, must be deplored by every Irishman who truly loves his country... The plough, the spade and the chisel have been employed in removing many of our prehistoric remains, because in this utilitarian age they have been considered impediments to modern improvements'.

– William Gray, 1883

Though it no longer exists, this monument is included because, as depicted in a rare early engraving, it shows just how impressive some of the larger undisturbed court tombs must have appeared. It stood in Killeevy parish below the eastern slope of Slieve Gullion, and was opened and explored by Sir Walter Synnot in 1791. Annacloghmullin did not survive long after discovery, most of its fine stones being carted away to build grand houses, but an account by John Bell published in *The Newry Magazine* in 1815 provides a valuable record of its structural features. His description of the gallery with its corbelled roof is particularly instructive. Thirty-seven feet in length, it contained four burial chambers (which he refers to as 'apartments') separated by sills: 'From the sides and ends of these apartments, springing from the top of the vertical wall-stones, large

flags which form the roof, project one over the other, until they nearly meet at the top, the stones at the ends converging as well as those of the sides. An immensely large and ponderous slab is placed horizontally on the two uppermost of these, which respective stones form the highest part of the several apartments'. The interior floor to roof height is given as 7½ feet.

The covering cairn, 44 yards long by 24 yards wide, was intact when dug into to expose the entrance to the tomb which, as the engraving shows, was flanked by a pair of massive orthostats. Similar flanking stones are still to be seen at Clontygora court tomb in the same county, the skeletal remains of which are perhaps the closest parallel to long-lost Annacloghmullin.

KILMALKEDAR

County Kerry

Prehistoric standing stones are to be found incorporated in a number of early monastic sites, and at Kilmalkedar, 4½ miles north-west of Dingle is this singularly slender hole stone which also bears an inscription in ogham along one side, dating this latter use of the stone to the early Christian period. At some point in its more recent history it came to be venerated for its reputed healing properties. Wakeman in *Archaeologia Hibernica* (1881) states that up to forty years previously its repute exceeded even that of the Stennis hole stone at Kirkwall in Orkney, and that it was 'believed by many of the old inhabitants of Kerry, that persons afflicted with chronic rheumatism, "falling sickness," or some other ills, might, by passing three times round it (with faith, and by offering certain prayers), be restored to health'. Similar miraculous powers were attributed to hole stones at Tobernaveen in Co. Sligo and Lackendarragh in Co. Cork.

CLOGHLEA

County Meath

This rare watercolour by antiquarian artist Gabriel Beranger is reproduced from the collection of his work held in the Royal Irish Academy in Dublin. It is the only record of an imposing megalithic structure at Cloghlea, Dowth, of which four massive standing stones remained at the time of his visit, in 1775. There are few clues as to its original form, but it is possibly the remains of an enormous stone circle that may once have surrounded a passage tomb mound. Beranger was clearly aware of the importance of recording these endangered ancient remains, and noted on his sketch pad: 'It stands on the edge of a quarry, so that in some time hence it is likely to be entirely demolished'. A single upright stone survived for much of the last century, but nothing now remains of this remarkable monument.

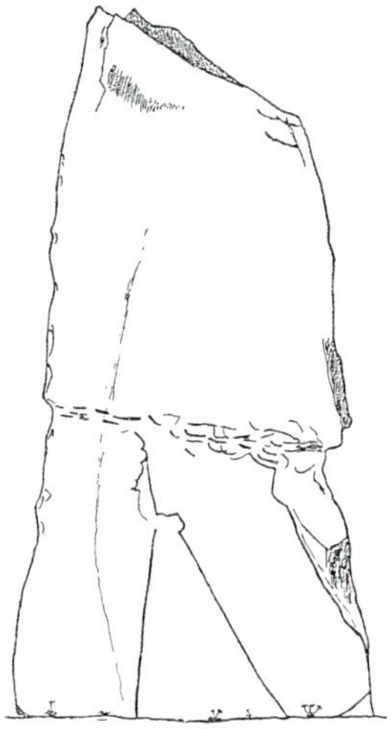

DRUMCOO

COUNTY FERMANAGH

Much mystery and folklore surrounds this curious stone, a 7 feet high limestone pillar situated in a field ½ mile north of Belcoo Bridge. It has been identified as the legendary pagan idol known as Crom Cruaich, which stood at Killinagh in the adjoining county of Cavan. Walter Harris wrote in 1739 of 'the celebrated idol of the Irish, called, *Crom Cruachd*, or the stone of Adoration, which stood in *Magh Sleachd*, i.e. the field of Worship, in the County of Cavan'. Tradition states that it was overthrown by St Patrick in the fifth century, and was removed to its present location to escape further attention from Christian missionaries.

The stone bears faint traces of carving in low relief, and one needs to peer closely to distinguish features said to represent a torso with girdle and tassel, and a pair of stumpy legs in striding attitude. It has been dated on no particular evidence to about 700 BC, but while this would be appropriate for the erection of the stone as an object of pagan veneration, it is almost certainly much too early for the execution of figure sculpture. Fermanagh is noted for a particular style of primitive figure carving attributable to the early Christian period, and it seems possible that the Drumcoo example is unfinished work of the genre, perhaps depicting a robed cleric similar to the smaller but more accomplished Bishop's Stone at Killadeas.

It could be significant that Killinagh, an area steeped in folklore and littered with relics of antiquity, lies only a couple of miles to the south-west, so the possibility that the stone was indeed brought thence cannot be ruled out. Whatever its provenance, its pagan overtones remain undiluted by attempts at conversion, or by exile to this secluded spot.

GOWARD

COUNTY DOWN

The excavation of this megalith, by Estyn Evans and Oliver Davies in 1932, marked a significant advance in local archaeology as the first thoroughly scientific investigation to be carried out on the earliest type of Neolithic burial monument: the court tombs, or Northern 'horned cairns' as they were initially termed. Almost four hundred examples have since been recorded and more than forty have been excavated.

Goward court tomb (which should not be confused with the better-known Goward dolmen in the same locality and described

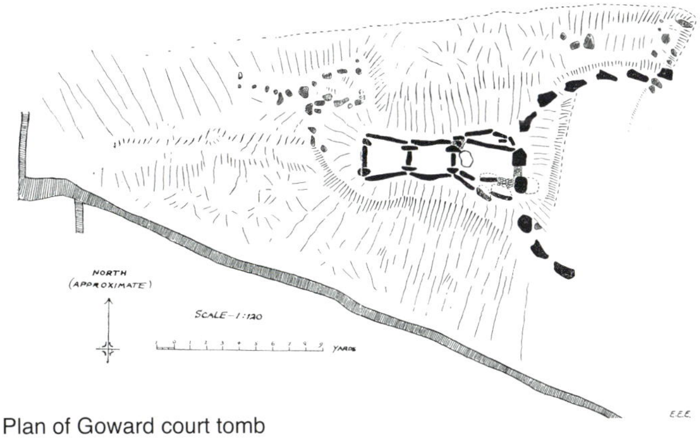

Plan of Goward court tomb

on *page 31*) lies near the top of Goward hill, 1¾ miles east-north-east of Hilltown. It is approached by a rough farm track leading steeply uphill to the north of the Bryansford road, then across two fields. The elevated site provides a good view of the Mourne Mountains to the south, and was evidently an important one for early man, for the surrounding area contains a number of unexplored cairns and mounds.

The tomb is uncared-for and the gallery is partly obscured by gorse; but the fine semi-circular forecourt of eleven large granite boulders, open-spaced rather than contiguous, stands out. At first sight it somewhat resembles a stone circle, and, 'with almost characteristic indifference to archaeological truth', had been recorded as such by the Ordnance Survey. A long tapered cairn measuring 115 feet east to west encloses a well constructed gallery of three chambers segmented by jambs and sills. The east (first) chamber is the largest and is set slightly askew to the others. It has the unusual feature of two outer rows of orthostats to provide additional support for a corbelled roof which no longer survives.

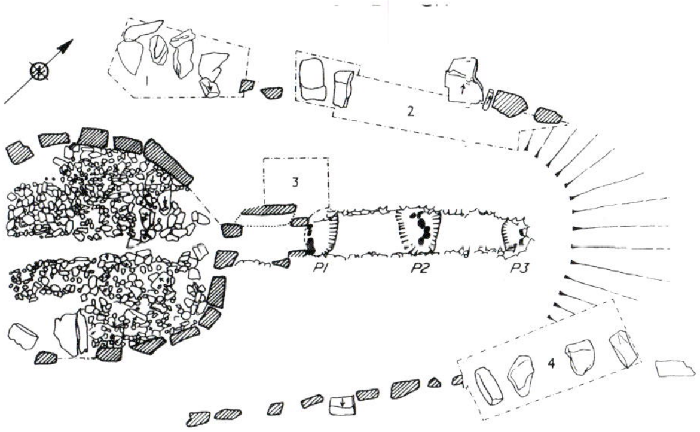

Above: Plan of the Ballymacaldrack court tomb. The long 'cremation passage' containing three circular pits lies behind the rectangular chamber opening off the U-shaped court

BALLYMACALDRACK

COUNTY ANTRIM

Ballymacaldrack, popularly known as Dooey's Cairn, is an accessible, well-preserved and in some important respects unusual example of a single court tomb. It stands in a fenced enclosure ¾ mile south-south-east of Dunloy village and is approached from a lane on the east side of Bellaghy road. Excavated by Estyn Evans in 1935 and by A. E. P. Collins in 1975, it figures frequently in the archaeological literature.

The megalith is contained in an ovoid-shaped cairn bounded by a substantial boulder kerb of which twenty-nine

stones survive. Several of the orthostats forming the deep U-shaped forecourt are impressive specimens; one flanking the chamber entrance stands over 6 feet tall. No evidence of burials was found in the small rectangular chamber which however yielded an array of ritual items. Its entrance had been closed with a panel of dry-walling between the jambs and in it were two polished stone axes, so-called 'magic guardians' of the tomb. Piled against this walling and extending across much of the court was a large amount of cairn material. Behind the chamber a long paved 'cremation passage' was uncovered (now completely grassed-over), where bodies were burned prior to depositing the bones in a series of pits dug in the floor. Dating evidence showed that this activity took place around 3500-3000 BC. The construction of the monument involved a number of separate phases and its use extended over several centuries, culminating in the symbolic sealing of the chamber and blocking of the court.

CRAIGAROGAN

COUNTY ANTRIM

Previously regarded as a passage tomb derivative but now generally accepted as a wedge tomb, this unusual megalith lies near the Ballymartin Water 200 yards north of the hamlet of Roughfort, which is 2½ miles east-south-east of Templepatrick. Though the main structural features survive it is in disarray and overgrown, with a formidable barrier of brambles along one side preventing close inspection. A plan drawn in the early 1900s shows a long boulder-built gallery covered by a series of roof-stones which decrease in height from front to back, typical of wedge tomb construction. Its east-north-east/west-south-west orientation is also consistent with the type, and so too is the

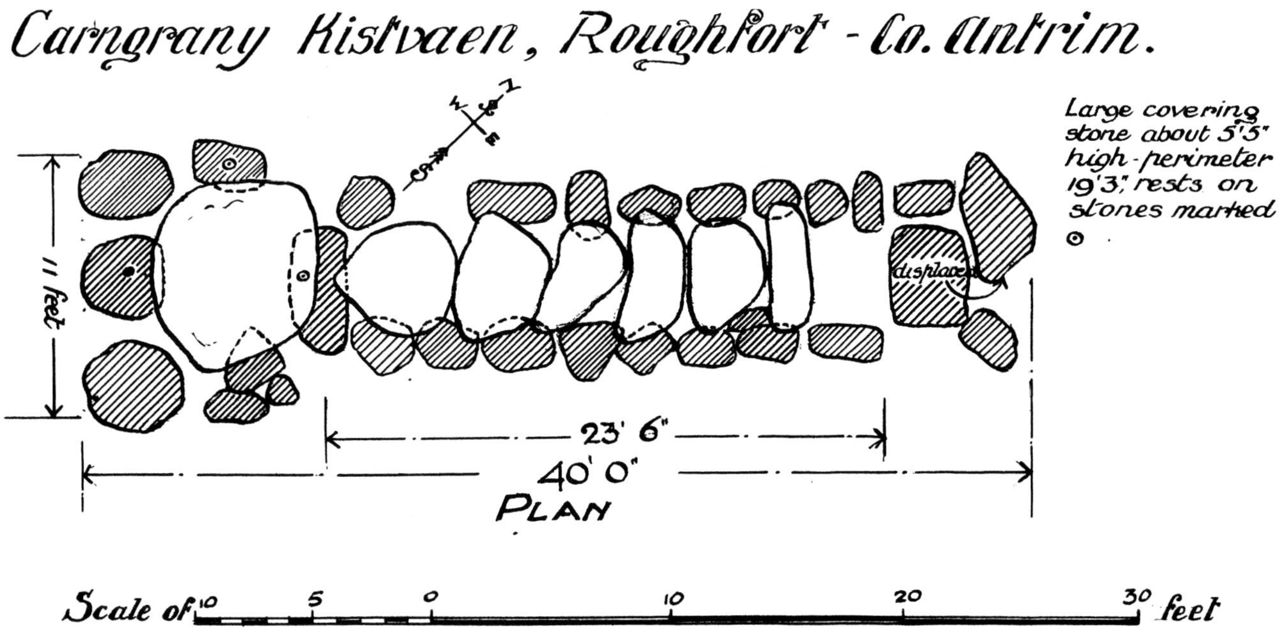

presence of an antechamber, which here takes the form of a dolmen-like structure in front of the gallery.

The Ordnance Survey Memoirs of 1838 state that 'within the memory of some old people this temple was enclosed by two circles of standing stones'. While the innermost was probably the kerb of a vanished cairn, it is possible that the outer one, which reportedly had a surrounding ditch, was a ritual feature, suggesting that this may have been a sacred site as well as a place of burial. A clue to its function may lie in the old name by which it is still known in the district: *Carn Greine,* 'Cairn of the Sun'. An encrusted urn recovered from the tomb early last century indicated a Bronze Age date for the monument, as would be expected.

Above: Plan of Craigarogan megalith

LEGANANNY

County Down

This famous megalith is the most recognisable in the north of Ireland. Its superb siting, on the lower slopes of Slieve Croob 4 miles south of Dromara, suggests that its builders had an eye for location: from it a panoramic view opens to the south with the entire sweep of the Mourne Mountains ranged across the horizon. The tomb well displays the sculptural qualities that define a 'tripod dolmen', a term coined by James Ferguson in the nineteenth century to describe this and similar portal tombs, believing that it never had a covering cairn and was always intended to be seen as it stands now, 'a studied exhibition of a *tour de force*'. In fact, there is some evidence for a cairn, though it is unlikely to have ever completely covered the structure and Ferguson was probably correct in his assumption. If proof were needed that Stone Age man built his monuments to instil awe as well as to endure, then it is surely to be found in the rugged granite geometry of Legananny, with its tall portal stones

lifting the 10½ feet-long tapered capstone clear against the sky. No recent excavations have been carried out, but old records refer to the discovery of urns here.

In the same townland is a fine Christianised standing stone of squarish appearance, 5 feet 9 inches high with a plain equal-armed cross inscribed on one side. The top of the stone is stepped or 'shouldered' in similar manner to the west portal stone of the dolmen.

Above: Dressed in finery more appropriate to a Victorian drawing-room than the stony slopes of Slieve Croob, the Countess Annesley and two Markham sisters pose on top of the famous Legananny dolmen during an excursion in the countryside. The photographer, probably Capt. H. Annesley, clearly had an eye for an unusual picture, and the ladies' evident agility in those long dresses calls for comment, but such frolics at an historic monument would be disapproved of today.

TICLOY

COUNTY ANTRIM

Above: Ticloy dolmen, from a nineteenth-century sketch
Inset: Plan of chamber

This distinctive small dolmen, 'The Stone House', stands little more than 6 feet in overall height at the east end of what appears to have been a long cairn, situated on the south side of Ticloy hill some 5 miles south-west of Carnlough. A neatly constructed chamber 4 feet square is roofed with two capstones and opens north-east between portal stones 5½ feet high, the southern of which lies fallen alongside. Its collapse was presumably the result of a treasure hunt over a century ago by the owner of the land, who boasted of having dreamt of a hoard of gold buried in the chamber. To his great disappointment – and it was said, much local glee – his only discovery after hours of fruitless digging, was an urn containing some burnt bones.

This megalith is of interest because of a plan in the 1830s *Ordnance Survey Memoirs*, which clearly shows that it had a curved orthostatic façade, traces of which survive, thus confirming a link with the court tombs. Portal tombs may have developed from court tombs and retained some of their features in a less elaborate form. Little remains of the cairn, and nothing at all of a second 'stone house' which once occupied its western end.

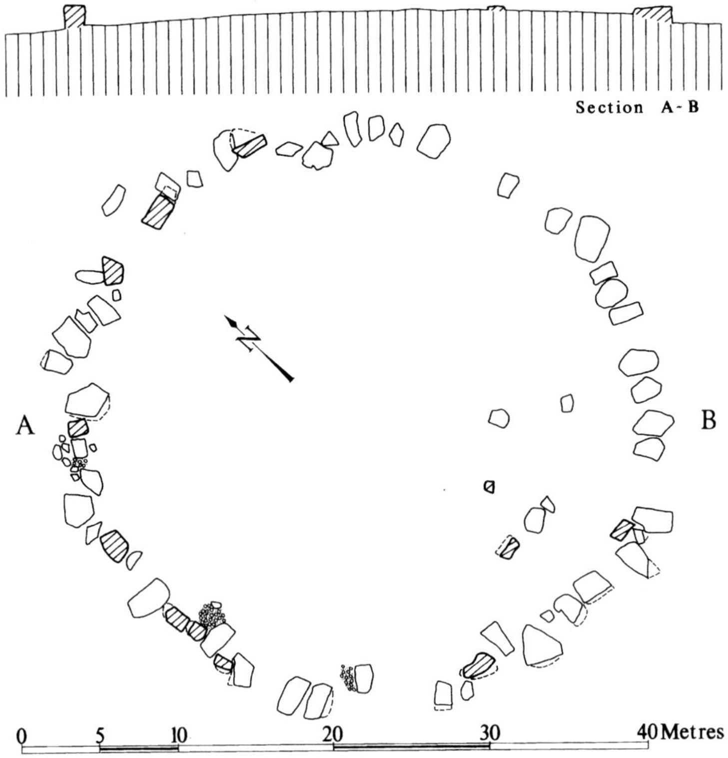

ANNAGHMORE GLEBE

COUNTY FERMANAGH

This 'Druid's Temple' was formerly regarded as a stone circle, but is now properly classified as the kerb of what was once a more complex monument. Its elevated siting, on an isolated drumlin ridge close to the Co. Cavan border, 4 miles south of Newtownbutler, suggests that it is a ransacked passage tomb, though no clear evidence of a burial chamber survives. A ring of massive stones placed end to end and measuring up to 6 feet in height, encloses an area 110 feet in diameter. The task of bringing them here would have required a large and highly organised workforce, so this was probably the tomb of someone of importance. It is clear from an early account that a sizeable structure did occupy the interior of the ring: a report in *The Fermanagh Times* of 14 May, 1891, quotes from a letter written to the Bishop of Clogher back in 1712, complaining that 'the heap has been removed to pave our ways and build that bridge'– a reference to Wattle Bridge, which the site overlooks.

Above: Plan and section

KILKEEL

County Down

This attractive but sadly neglected little dolmen, 'The Crawtree Stone', stands little more than 6 feet high and is almost concealed by a hedge in a private lane ¼ mile north-east of Kilkeel. Its name is said to derive from *cruit*, meaning a hump, which is a fair description of the rotund capstone measuring some 8 feet across. An unsightly field fence has been erected in front of the chamber entrance but its structural features can be seen well enough. The convex underside of the capstone is neatly cradled by four low uprights, two of which are the well matched portal stones facing south-west. The chamber is open at the rear and if there ever was a backstone it may have been removed when the laneway was made. Furthermore, a boulder set between the portal stones does not seem to be a normal sillstone. Given the disruption around it, it is perhaps fortunate to have survived to the extent it has. Like most megaliths in the Mournes district it is built of granite, and many less accessible monuments have been plundered for their stones.

At Dunnaman, 1 mile due west, an interesting four-chambered gallery is all that remains of a large court tomb; and 4 miles further on towards Rostrevor is Kilfeaghan dolmen, a portal tomb with a massive 35-ton capstone.

GLENKNOCK

County Tyrone

'The Druid's Altar' is a ruined but still impressive megalith, 1½ miles north-north-east of Newtownstewart in Glenknock (or Cloghogle) townland. It occupies a slightly elevated site in pastureland to the east side of Gallon road, about 600 yards south-west of Gallon bridge. The massive capstone, originally 9 feet long, fell about twenty-five years ago and now lies broken in several large pieces among the chamber stones, which are themselves in disarray. An archaeological field sketch made earlier last century depicts a fine dolmen structure whose collapse is all the more regrettable since it may have been preventable, apparently having occurred at the time of a land reclamation scheme, though frost damage cannot be ruled out as a possible cause. The plan of the chamber is unclear, but the table-like capstone was raised aloft on just three uprights – a pair of portal stones oriented north-west, and a backstone – so one might class this as a tripod dolmen. A tall stone which stood at one side of the entrance may have been a remnant of a forecourt, indicating a cultural link between court and portal tombs. The surrounding cairn has largely been obliterated by ploughing.

CROSH

County Tyrone

Scarcely ½ mile east of the previous entry, in the adjoining townland of Crosh, is another dolmen splendidly situated on a grassy eminence behind a farm on Carnargan road, 1½ miles north-east of Newtownstewart. Like its neighbour in Glenknock it is partly collapsed. Even so, this is a spectacular megalith on account of the colossal portal stones, 8 feet tall, flanking a doorstone rising to half their height. On present evidence the chamber, 15 feet long externally and oriented towards east, appears to have been covered by three capstones, all displaced. Only one sidestone survives and the backstone is missing. Erosion at the base of the north portal has exposed a packing stone which is in danger of giving way under pressure from the slipped capstone. Remains of the cairn can be seen around the chamber.

Access to the monument, formerly by a short laneway directly opposite the junction of Carnargan and Crosh roads, is now blocked by a barbed-wire fence, and permission to approach it through the farmyard should be sought at the house.

DUNNAMORE

County Tyrone

'Dermot and Grania's Bed' is a large and somewhat damaged Bronze Age wedge tomb situated in the hamlet of Dunnamore, 8 miles west-south-west of Cookstown. The recommended approach is by a farm track leading west from a concreted lane to the south of the road; the megalith comes into view beside some trees in the next field. Despite obvious disturbance and the removal of a number of its stones, the tomb is a good example of the class. The largest in the county, with a well-defined gallery which still has several massive roof slabs in place, it consists of an antechamber and main chamber, 9 feet and 15 feet long respectively, divided by a high septal slab. An unusual though not unique feature is the presence of an orthostat set midway between the portals, creating a kind of dual entrance. It is structurally unnecessary, so is presumably of ritual significance. Some of the outer walling survives, much confused by agricultural activity. The tomb occupies a fine location, modern intrusions notwithstanding, and the south-west facing entrance looks out across a wide sweep of largely uninterrupted countryside.

SLIEVE NA CALLIAGH

COUNTY MEATH

Sliabh na Callighe translates as 'Hill of the Witch' the hag goddess of ancient legend, and is the name given to this sprawling megalithic cemetery of about thirty passage tombs occupying three summits – Carnbane East, Carnbane West and Patrickstown – in the Loughcrew hills, 10 miles west of Kells. Many of the monuments are in a poor state of preservation, most have been plundered and only one has been the subject of scientific investigation (Cairn H, in 1943). The letters by which the cairns are identified today are the same as used by Eugene Conwell in his 1860s survey. One of the best preserved tombs is Cairn T on Carnbane East. It is also the largest here, providing a focal point for six smaller tombs grouped about it. 'Carnbane' means 'white cairn', and it is known from old records that Cairn T formerly had a cladding of white quartz rising above its kerb of massive stones. A short passage leads into a cruciform chamber, comprising a large central area with three side chambers, many of whose stones are richly decorated with a range of motifs. The western summit also has a dominant tomb, Cairn K, which has an elaborate chamber with five side chambers, again bearing decoration, also a fine pillarstone of ritual significance. The majority of the Loughcrew tombs were probably built in the late Neolithic period, about 3000-2500 BC.

TAWNATRUFFAUN

COUNTY SLIGO

'The Giant's Griddle' is a well-preserved portal tomb of classic form, sited in the Easky river valley 5 miles south-west of Dromore West. The townland name has been translated as 'the grassy height by the stream' (the Fiddangarrode, which is close by). The land here is rough and marshy, especially after periods of rain, so sturdy footwear is advisable when exploring. A field wall has been built alongside the monument, fortunately without serious detriment, though at least one chamber stone and many smaller cairn stones seem to have been appropriated for the purpose. The tomb is a clean-cut example of its type and should perhaps be described as a 'tripod dolmen'. A pair of 5-feet high portal stones support the leading edge of the oversailing capstone, the back end of which rests, with only the merest contact, on the tip of a single upright.

KILNARUANE

County Cork

'The Bantry Pillar', as this 7-feet high monolith is generally known, surmounts a low earthen platform on a hill crest 1 mile west-south-west of Bantry. It is decorated on one face with weathered scriptural scenes, and on the other with a carving of a primitive boat and crew. Mortises on either side of the dressed pillar were probably intended to hold the horizontal arms of a cross, so this monument possibly represents an early stage in the evolution of the tall free-standing High Crosses from Christianised standing stones and cross-slabs, and as such could date from the eighth century or before.

Glossary

Alignment A group of standing stones, usually numbering from three to six, arranged in a straight row, sometimes occurring in association with stone circles.
Antechamber A short fore-chamber typical of wedge tombs, separated from the main chamber of the gallery by an upright slab. If open at the front, it may be referred to as a portico.
Anthropomorphic Having the appearance of human form, sometimes applied to standing stones.
Axial stone Also referred to as a recumbent stone, a feature of stone circles in south-west Ireland, associated with orientation.
Baetyl Small water-smoothed boulder, oval in shape, found in some prehistoric burials.
Boulder tomb A Bronze Age burial monument resembling a diminutive dolmen crouching close to the ground, with a rounded capstone resting on three or four low boulders. Sometimes found at the centre of a stone circle.
Cairn or 'Carn' in Irish place names, a mound of stones raised over a megalithic tomb to provide a covering and also hold the roof corbelling in place. When constructed of earth it is called a tumulus.
Capstone A large slab or boulder covering the chamber of a megalithic tomb. A particularly striking feature of portal tombs.
Corbel A method of roofing employed in several types of megalithic tomb, consisting of overlapping slabs of stone rising above the sidestones of the chamber and continuing upwards to converge at the top. The technique is seen at its most sophisticated in the great chamber at Newgrange.
Court tomb Earliest type of Neolithic tomb, consisting of a long gallery segmented by jambs into several chambers, opening onto a semi-circular façade of standing stones forming a forecourt. The court can take forms other than semi-circular: Full-court, an oval enclosure with entrance at the end furthest from the gallery; Central-court, having opposing galleries opening off each end; Dual-court, in essence two court tombs set back to back in the same long cairn. Court tombs are concentrated overwhelmingly in the northern half of the country.
Cromlech Old-fashioned and inaccurate nineteenth-century name for a dolmen.
Cup-marks Small saucer-like depressions decorating the surface of a stone, sometimes surrounded by single or multiple rings – 'cup-and-ring marks'.
Dolmen Popular name for a portal tomb, derived from the Breton word for a stone table.
Double-walling A defining feature of most wedge tombs, this is an outer row of orthostats running parallel with the side walls of the gallery at a distance of several feet.
Dry-walling Masonry built up course upon course without mortar, a feature of some megalithic tombs.
Fosse A ditch dug round the inside of an earth-banked enclosure or stone circle, usually associated with henge monuments.
Gallán/Dallán The Irish name for a standing stone, also known as a *menhir*.
Henge A ritual enclosure or sanctuary comprising an earthen ring-bank with internal ditch, or 'fosse'. Some have megalithic elements, like Reanascreena in Co. Cork which surrounds a stone circle, and The Giant's Ring near Belfast, with a dolmen at its centre.
Jambs Paired orthostats placed to divide the gallery of a court tomb into a series of individual chambers, usually with an upright slab set between them.
Kerb A revetment of stones retaining cairn material in place. They may be set upright, or laid horizontally. Exceptionally massive kerb stones are a notable feature of the great passage tombs of the Boyne Valley.
La Tène Highly distinctive Iron Age decoration, characterised by stylised curvilinear designs.
Lintel A horizontal roofing stone, particularly at the entrance to a tomb chamber.
Megalithic tomb By definition, a prehistoric tomb built of large stones; it is however also used to describe tombs which utilise quite small stones in a form of construction known as dry-walling, but which belong to the same 'megalithic tradition'.
Ogham Early Irish script derived from the Latin alphabet, consisting of groups of lines representing characters, inscribed across and on either side of a stem line, usually the sharp edge of a standing stone. The inscriptions are nearly always commemorative and date to the early Christian period.

Orthostat Any upright stone forming part of a megalithic tomb.
Passage tomb A tomb whose burial chamber is accessed by a lintel-roofed passage leading in from the side of the cairn. They are typically sited on hilltops. Some Ulster examples lack a passage but belong to the same class of monument.
Pattern A gathering or pilgrimage in honour of a saint's day.
Portal stones A pair of orthostats flanking the entrance to the chamber of a megalithic tomb. The most imposing are found in dolmens and may reach heights of 10 feet or more.
Portal tomb A single-chamber megalithic tomb of often dramatic appearance, whose characteristic feature is a large capstone oversailing the entrance formed by a pair of tall portal stones. They were built in the late Neolithic period and may have evolved from the court tombs.
Portico Porch-like entrance of some wedge tombs, and in dolmens whose doorstone is recessed behind the portals.
Post-and-panel Method of construction employed in some court tombs, whereby sections of dry-walling are inserted to bridge gaps between large upright stones.
Standing stone The simplest and most ubiquitous of all megalithic monuments, a single upright stone serving a variety of purposes. They are closely associated with the Bronze Age, though the custom of erecting them must have begun much earlier as they are given positions of prominence in some passage tombs, presumably as sacred symbols.
Stone circle A ring of spaced standing stones whose purpose was essentially ritual. Orientation also appears to have been a significant factor in their construction. A particular type, frequent in south-west Munster, is known as a recumbent or axial stone circle, one of whose stones is laid horizontally at the opposite side of the ring to the dominant portal stones, providing a specific astronomical alignment.
Stone pair Similar to an 'alignment' but consisting of only two stones set a short distance apart. Some are thought to be male and female representations.
Wedge tomb A megalithic tomb whose name is descriptive of its overall shape, tapering in height and width from front to back. The tomb entrance almost invariably faces between west and south-west, a similar orientation to many stone circles with which the type is broadly contemporary. Wedge tombs were introduced at the end of the Neolithic period and continued to be built in the Bronze Age. They are found throughout Ireland and are particularly numerous in the Burren region of Co. Clare.

BIBLIOGRAPHY

An Archaeological Survey of County Down, 1966

Beattie, S. *Ancient Monuments of Inishowen*, 1992

Benn, G. *History of the Town of Belfast*, Belfast, 1823

Bord Failte. *Bord Failte Ireland Guide*, Dublin 2000

Borlase, W.C. *The Dolmens of Ireland*, 3 Vols., London, 1897

Brash, R.H. *The Ogam Inscribed Monuments of the Gaedhil in the British Islands*, London, 1879

Brennan, J.H. *A Guide to Megalithic Ireland*, London, 1994

Brennan, M. *The Stars and the Stones: Ancient Art and Astronomy in Ireland*, London, 1983

Buckley, V.M. *Archaeological Inventory of County Louth*, Stationery Office, Dublin, 1986

Burl, A. *The Stone Circles of the British Isles*, Newhaven and London, 1976

Burl, A. *Rings of Stone*, London, 1979

Burl, A. 'The sun, the moon and megaliths: archaeoastronomy and the standing stones of Northern Ireland' *Ulster Journal of Archaeology*, 50, 1987, 7-21

Burl, A. *A Guide to the Stone Circles of Britain, Ireland and Brittany*, Yale, 1995

Chart, D.A., Evans, E.E., Lawlor, H.C. (ed), *A Preliminary Survey of the Ancient Monuments of Northern Ireland*, H.M.S.O., 1940

Collins, A.E.P. 'Excavations at the Giant's Ring, Ballynahatty', *Ulster Journal of Archaeology*, 20, 1957, 44-50

Collins, A.E.P. 'Dooey's Cairn, Ballymacaldrack, Co. Antrim, *Ulster Journal of Archaeology*, 39, 1976, 1-7

Cooney, G. *Landscapes of Neolithic Ireland*, London, 2000

Cromwell, T. *Excursions Through Ireland*, 1820

Davies, O. 'Stone Circles in Northern Ireland', *Ulster Journal of Archaeology*, 2, 1939, 2-14

de Valéra, R. 'The Court Cairns of Ireland', *Proceedings of the Royal Irish Academy*, 60c, 1959-60, 9-140

de Valéra, R. & Ó Nualláin, S. *Survey of the Megalithic Tombs of Ireland*, Vol. 1, Co. Clare, 1961; Vol. 2, Co. Mayo, 1964; Vo1. 3, Cos. Galway, Roscommon, Leitrim, Cavan, Longford, Westmeath, 1972; Vol. 4, Cos. Cork & Kerry, 1982

de Valéra, R, and O'Nuallain, S. 'The Megalithic Tombs of the Island of Achill', *Journal of the Royal Society of Antiquaries of Ireland*, 20, 1950

Donnelly, C.J. *Archaeology, Continuity and Change at Historic Monuments in Northern Ireland*, Belfast, 1997

Dubourdieu, W.J. *Statistical Survey of the County of Antrim*, 1802; *County Down*, 1812

Evans, E.E. *The Personality of Ireland*, Belfast, 1981

Evans, E.E. *Prehistoric and Early Christian Ireland*, London, 1966

Ferguson, J. *Rude Stone Monuments in All Countries*, London, 1872

Flanaghan, L. *Ancient Ireland: Life Before the Celts*, Dublin, 1998

Gray, W. 'The Cromlechs of Antrim and Down', *Proceedings of the Belfast Natural History and Philosophical Society*, 1883-4, 225

Hamlin, A. *Historic Monuments of Northern Ireland*, Belfast, 1983

Harbison, P. *The Archaeology of Ireland*, London, 1976

Harbison, P. *Pre-Christian Ireland*, London, 1988

Harbison, P. *Beranger's Views of Ireland*, Royal Irish Academy, Dublin, 1991

Harbison, P. *Guide to the National Monuments of Ireland*, Dublin, 1992

Harbison, P. *Beranger's Rambles in Ireland*, Bray, Co. Wicklow, 2004

Hartwell, B. 'Ballynahatty - a prehistoric ceremonial centre', *Archaeology Ireland*, 18, 1991, 12-15

Herity, M. Gleanncholmcille: *A Guide to 5,000 years of History in Stone*, Dublin 1998

Herity, M. *Irish Passage Graves*, Dublin, 1974

Herity, M. & Eogan, G. *Ireland in Prehistory*, London, 1977

Kennedy, C. *Ancient Ireland, The User's Guide*, Killala, 1997

Killanin, Lord, & Duignan, M.V. *The Shell Guide to Ireland*, Dublin, 1989, revised and updated by Peter Harbinson, London, 1989

Lacy, B. (ed.) *Archaeological Survey of County Donegal*, Donegal County Council, Lifford, 1983

Ledwich, E. *Antiquities of Ireland*, 1790

McCombs Guide to Belfast, Belfast, 1861

Macalister, R.A.S. *The Archaeology of Ireland*, London, 1949

Meehan, C. *The Traveller's Guide to Sacred Ireland*, Glastonbury, 2002

Mallory, J.P. & McNeill, T.E. *The Archaeology of Ulster*, Belfast, 1991, 1995

Marshall, J.D.C. *Forgotten places of the North Coast*, Armoy, Co.

Antrim, 1987, 1991
Movius, H.L. *The Irish Stone Age*, Cambridge, 1942
Newenham, R. O'C. *Picturesque Views of the Antiquities of Ireland*, Vol. 2, 1830
O'Kelly, M.T. *Newgrange: Archaeology, Art and Legend*, London, 1982
O'Kelly, M.J. *Early Ireland*, Cambridge, 1989
O'Neill, H. 'The Rock Monuments of the County of Dublin', *Transactions of the Kilkenny Archaeological Society*, 1852, 40
Ó Nualláin, S. *Stone Circles in Ireland*, Dublin, 1995
O'Sullivan, M. *Megalithic Art in Ireland*, Dublin, 1993
Otway, C. *A Tour in Connaught*, Dublin, 1839
Poe, J.W. *Cromlechs of County Dublin*, Dublin, *c.*1909
Raftery, J. *Prehistoric Ireland*, London, 1951
Ríordáin, S.P. *Antiquities of the Irish Countryside*, London, 1987
Roberts, J. *Exploring West Cork*, Skibbereen, 1988
Roberts, J. *The Stone Circles of Cork and Kerry: An Astronomical Guide*
Ross, A. *Pagan Celtic Britain*, London, 1967
Shee, T. *Irish Megalithic Tombs*, Shire Books, 1990
Somerville, B.T. 'Five Stone Circles in West Cork', *Journal of the Cork Historical and Archaeological Society*, 35, 1930, 70
Streit, J. *Sun and Cross*, 1977
The Newry Magazine, July-August, 1815
Wakeman, W.F. *Handbook of Irish Antiquities*, 1848
Ware, Sir J., Ed. Harris, W. *The History and Antiquities of Ireland*, London, 1739
Weir, A. *Early Ireland: a Field Guide*, Belfast, 1980
Wilde, Sir W. *Lough Corrib, its Shores and Islands*, Dublin, 1867
Wood-Martin, W.G. *Pagan Ireland*, London, 1895
Wood-Martin, W.G. *The Rude Stone Monuments of Ireland*, London, 1888

ACKNOWLEDGEMENTS

A book of this kind necessarily draws on accumulated knowledge from many sources: guide books old and new; historical references and memoirs; archaeological surveys and specialist journals; and my indebtedness to these is conveyed though the bibliography.

I must also thank a number of individuals who assisted in various ways, particularly Michael Manning, tourism officer for the West Cork region, who unerringly guided me to several elusive sites. To Peter Harbison I am grateful for bringing to my attention the treasury of antiquarian watercolours by Gabriel Beranger housed in the Royal Irish Academy, whose librarian Siobhan Fitzpatrick kindly allowed me to photograph relevant items from the collection. For their ever-courteous response to enquiries and generally facilitating my research, I wish to acknowledge the contribution of the following: John Killen and staff, Linen Hall Library, Belfast; Fergal Martin, Office of Public Works (National Monuments), Dublin; Claire Tuffy and colleagues at Brú na Bóinne, Donore; Gail Pollock and Robert Hadden, Environment and Heritage Service of Northern Ireland; Trevor Caughey, Fáilte Ireland; Trustees of the Ulster Museum; The Royal Society of Antiquaries of Ireland; Belfast Central Library; Public Record Office of Northern Ireland.

The megalithic trail leads in diverse and often unexpected directions, and I here express my gratitude to the many country folk I met on my rambles, who set me on the right track on numerous occasions and sometimes quite literally went out of their way to be of help.

No book is exclusively the work of an individual; at some point its realisation becomes the product of many hands and I am indebted to Appletree Press for its enthusiastic commitment to this project, by its director John Murphy who commissioned it, and in production by editor Jean Brown and designer Stuart Wilkinson for their proficiency in bringing it all together.

INDEX TO SITES

CREDITS

Additional illustrations are from the following sources:

Abbreviations

PRIA Proceedings of the Royal Irish Academy
EHSNI The Monuments and Buildings Record of Environment and Heritage Service, Northern Ireland
JRSAI Journal of the Royal Society of Antiquaries in Ireland

Page
27 Plan of Beaghmore stone circle complex. Supplied by EHSNI
29 Wedge tomb at Paddock, Co. Louth. *JRSAI* 5, 1864-66, 498
30 Plan of Longstone Rath, Co. Kildare. *PRIA* 30 C, 1912-13, P1.XXXIX
32 Dolmen at Goward, Co. Down. Plan by the author after an original supplied by EHSNI
33 Dolmen at Kiltiernan, Co. Dublin. From a watercolour by Gabriel Beranger, Royal Irish Academy Ms. 3.C.30
34 Frontispiece: *The Triumph and Passing of Cúchulainn*, by Standish O'Grady, 1920
37 Griddle-More-na-Vean, Co. Sligo. *JRSAI* 1887, 288
40 Dolmen at Kilmogue, Co. Waterford. *Archaeologica*, Vol. XVI, P1.18
42 Hole Stone at Tobernavean, Co. Sligo. *JRSAI* 8, 1887, 74
48 Pillarstone at Doonfeeny, Co. Mayo. *JRSAI* 42, 1912, 114
52 Dolmen at Woodtown, Co. Dublin. From a watercolour by Gabriel Beranger, Royal Irish Academy Ms. 3.C.30
53 Dolmen at Brenanstown, Co. Dublin. From a watercolour by Gabriel Beranger, Royal Irish Academy Ms. 3.C.30
54 (Top) The Druid's Altar, Ballylumford, Co. Antrim. *The Dublin Penny Journal*, 29 December, 1832
54 (Bottom) *Proceedings of the Belfast Naturalists Field Club*, 1883-4, 225
61 Dolmen at Churchtown, Co. Tyrone. *JRSAI* 12, 1872-3, 526
63 Clonfinlough Stone, Co. Offaly. *JRSAI* 5, 1864-66, 361
64 The Long Stones, Aghmakane, Co. Armagh. Plan and section by the author after an original sketch supplied by EHSNI
66 Dolmen at Ballynageeragh, Co. Waterford. *JRSAI* 5, 1864-66, 480
68 The Broad Stone, Co. Antrim. Plan by the author after an original supplied by EHSNI
70 Plan of Creevykeel court tomb, Co. Sligo. *JRSAI* 69, 1939, 53
71 Conjectural reconstruction of wedge tomb at Island, Co. Cork. E. Fahy, *JRSAI* 88, 1958, 20
75 Plan of cairn at Millin Bay, Co. Down. Supplied by EHSNI
79 Plan and section of chamber, Cairn K, Carrowkeel, Co. Sligo. *PRIA* 29 C, 1911-12, P1.XXI
82 Pillarstone at Kilnasaggart, Co. Armagh. From *Tours in Ulster* by J. B. Doyle, 1854
91 Plan of Ballynoe stone circle, Co. Down. Supplied by EHSNI
94 (Top) Dolmen at Proleek, Co. Louth. From *Louthiana* by Thomas Wright, 1748
94 (Bottom) Dolmen at Proleek, Co. Louth. From *Picturesque Views of the Antiquities of Ireland* by R. O'C Newenham, 1830
95 Dolmen at Howth, Co. Dublin. *JRSAI* 2, 1852, 40
97 Plan of Annaghmare court tomb, Co. Armagh. Supplied by EHSNI
100 Plan of Boviel wedge tomb, Co. Londonderry. Supplied by EHSNI
104 Plan of Slieve Gullion passage tomb, Co. Armagh. Supplied by EHSNI
106 Stone Circle near Cong. Co. Mayo. From *Lough Corrib* by Sir William Wilde, 1867
110 Dolmen at Haroldstown, Co. Carlow. Plan by the author after *JRSAI* 71, 1941, 18
111 Plan of Labbacallee wedge tomb, Co. Cork. *PRIA* 43 C, 1936, P1.XII
114 (Right) Plan and section of Kilfeaghan dolmen, Co. Down. Supplied by EHSNI
114 (Left) Plan of Giant's Ring, Co. Down. Supplied by EHSNI
115 Court tomb at Annaghcloghmullin, Co. Armagh. *The Newry Magazine*, Vol. 1, July/August 1815
117 Megalithic structure at Cloghlea, Co. Meath. From a watercolour by Gabriel Beranger, Royal Irish Academy Ms. 3.C.30
118 Sketch of Crom Cruaich standing stone at Drumcoo, Co. Fermanagh. Supplied by EHSNI
119 Court tomb at Goward, Co. Down. Plan by E. Evans, supplied by EHSNI
121 Plan of Ballymacaldrack court tomb, Co. Antrim. Supplied by EHSNI
123 (Top) Wedge tomb at Craigarogan, Co. Antrim. Plan supplied by EHSNI
123 (Bottom) Woodcut from *History of the Town of Belfast* by G. Benn, 1823
126 Photograph of Legananny dolmen, Co. Down, *c.* 1880. Reproduced by kind permission of The Public Record Office of Northern Ireland (Ref. D1854/5/5/84), and The Trustees of the Museums and Galleries of N.I.
127 Dolmen at Ticloy, Co. Antrim. From *Dolmens of Ireland* Vol. 1, by W. C. Borlase, 1887, 266. (inset) Plan by the author after an original by E. Evans, supplied by EHSNI
128 Plan of Annaghmore Glebe, Co. Fermanagh. Supplied by EHSNI
133 Chamber of Cairn K, Slieve na Calliagh, Co. Meath. *JRSAI* 5, 1864-66, 354